Growth In Ministry

Contributors

WILLMAR THORKELSON is Religion Editor for the *Minneapolis Star* and is widely recognized as one of the best journalists in the religious field.

MARVIN JOHNSON was a member of the Growth in Ministry research staff and currently teaches at California Lutheran College.

JOSEPH WAGNER directed the Growth in Ministry Project and is on the staff of the Division for Professional Leadership of the Lutheran Church in America.

JAMES DITTES teaches in the Yale University Department of Religious Studies. He was a consultant to the Growth in Ministry Project.

HAROLD LOHR is a member of the staff of the Lutheran Church in America's Division for Professional Leadership and served on the Growth in Ministry team.

IRENE LOVETT, a psychologist, is an ordained minister in the American Baptist Church. She has served in the parish but more recently was Director and Career Development Counselor at the American Baptist Church Center in Wellesley Hills, Massachusetts.

GRANGER WESTBERG is a Lutheran pastor on the faculty of the University of Illinois Medical School and directs an innovative research project in preventative medicine through Wholistic Health Centers located in Chicago area churches. He is also a noted author.

PETER STEINKE is a parish pastor in the Lutheran Church—Missouri Synod. He is the author of numerous books and articles and is a trainer for the Pastor as Teacher Workshops.

MARK ROUCH is the director of the Intentional Growth Center at Lake Junalaska, N.C., and conducts continuing education and career development and evaluation programs there. He is a frequent writer and public speaker.

DAVID MARTIN is an administrative assistant to the President of the North Carolina Synod of the Lutheran Church in America. He has been actively involved in counseling with pastors and their families and has designed and directed numerous retreats for pastors and spouses.

THOMAS E. KADEL is a Lutheran Church in America pastor in the Upper Dublin Lutheran Church in Ambler, Pa. He has frequently written for synod and church-wide publications.

Growth In Ministry

Edited by
THOMAS E. KADEL

FORTRESS PRESS   PHILADELPHIA

Biblical quotations from the Revised Standard Version of the Bible, copyrighted 1946, 1952, © 1971, 1973 by the Division of Christian Education of the National Council of the Churches of Christ in the U.S.A., are used by permission.

Library of Congress Cataloging in Publication Data
Main entry under title:

Growth in ministry.

    Includes bibliographical references.
    1. Pastoral theology—Addresses, essays, lectures.
2. Pastoral theology—Lutheran Church—Addresses, essays, lectures. I. Kadel, Thomas E.
BV4011.G77   253   79–8902
ISBN 0–8006–1383–X

8029J79   Printed in the United States of America   1–1383

Contents

Editor's Foreword

Things don't grow all by themselves. Even the simple single-celled animals need nourishment and the proper ecological system in order to grow and reproduce. The more complex the organism, the more necessary it is for an increasing number of conditions to be "right" before growth occurs. Growth is not a given of life.

Growth is not a given of ministry either. It cannot be taken for granted. Yet, it often is. The average minister likely spends more time and money each year keeping the automobile running than in nurturing the conditions for professional growth.

The same can likely be said for most congregations. It is common for congregations to consume many more of their resources maintaining the building than in growing in their total ministry.

In the mid-seventies a major grant from Aid Association for Lutherans, a fraternal insurance company, made possible a very comprehensive study of pastoral effectiveness and satisfaction. This was something of a pulse-taking effort designed to learn what kind of growth was being experienced by Lutheran clergy and what growth-enabling and growth-inhibiting factors were generally present.

The Growth in Ministry Project was initiated by the Lutheran Church in America and the Lutheran Church—Missouri Synod. The American Lutheran Church participated in selected portions of the project after its initial phase. The research information was gathered in a representative sample of four hundred congregations. It sought information about pastoral effectiveness from congregational members, pastors, and pastors' spouses. It also tried to learn about levels of satisfaction in the ministry from the clergy. In all, nearly four thousand persons were surveyed.

When the study ended, the raw data filled a 172-page report. The churches have used the data to design a series of workshops for pastors and others to deal with the more significant issues which surfaced. To date, seven of these workshops have been offered, including Model A, Spiritual Growth, Pastor as Teacher, Shared Ministry, Support Systems, Preretirement, and Growth in Marriage.

This book, named after the study, addresses several of the study's discoveries. Note, however, this is not an attempt to discuss all the major functions of ministry, but rather to share and comment on some of the more important of the study's discoveries.

We asked our writers to share their ideas about these discoveries. For example, when counseling did *not* end up as a separate pastoral role, we went to Granger Westberg and asked why.

The writers' comments are not to be considered the last word on any of these subjects. Readers may disagree with some ideas in each chapter. That's as it should be, for our purpose is to provide the proverbial grist for the mill and not to tell anyone how they should think. To that end, there is a brief editor's note preceding each chapter which includes the specific question we asked of the writer and some comments on the writer's ideas.

With all of this said, however, let's get back to the notion of growth. Neither the study nor this book is of much value if it does not help pastors and their people to grow in the ministry they share together.

Growth is an expanding and a maturing; a process rather than an event. The old line is true—"When you stop growing, you start dying." Sometimes growth is quite painful and other times it can be exhilarating. But almost always it involves some risk, some casting off of the old and familiar and rewrapping oneself in new garments.

This book is an invitation to begin or to intensify growth in ministry. You may simply read it and perhaps have mental debates with the writers. Or it might be useful as a study and discussion resource for clergy groups, church councils, or pastoral relations committees.

However the book is used, we hope that it will be helpful in assisting growth in your ministry.

Tom Kadel

Recently, an older pastor, about to retire, said, "I'm glad I'm retiring. I'm not sure I understand what the ministry is any more." Has the ministry really changed that much in the postwar period? Nearly everyone would have some kind of opinion about this. Three of the more significant opinions (at least for Lutherans) would be those of the major church presidents. We sent Willmar Thorkelson out with pad and pencil to talk to Dr. James R. Crumley, Jr., of the Lutheran Church in America, Dr. Jacob A. O. Preus of the Lutheran Church—Missouri Synod, and Dr. David W. Preus of the American Lutheran Church. Their ideas of where we've been and where we're heading are significant because their perceptions no doubt color their administrations. But no less importantly, a parish pastor's impressions of these same forces of history and future will color the ministry he or she offers to a congregation and community.—*Editor*

1

The Postwar Pastorate: A Conversation with the Church Presidents

WILLMAR THORKELSON

Lutheran pastors, like other clergy, may no longer enjoy the status with the public they once had, but the expectations of lay Lutherans for their ministry have never been higher.

Ministry has changed in the past three decades because of vast changes in society. And the future may require continued change in the direction and emphasis of pastoral ministry, although its functions will remain basically the same.

That is the collective assessment of the presidents of the three major Lutheran bodies in the United States and Canada as the decade of the seventies wound to a close.

After noting how the pastoral ministry has changed since World War II, the church presidents looked ahead to the 1980s and beyond to predict what directions the ministry will be taking and which partial functions they expect to become increasingly important.

Dr. James R. Crumley, Jr., president of the Lutheran Church in America (LCA), said that the past three decades have been so different that you could say the ministry in each of them has also been different, even though the functions have been the same.

"In the 1950s," he pointed out, "pastoral ministry was easy in the sense that it was met with acceptance. There was a positive attitude toward the church, and pastors didn't feel they always had to be explaining themselves or apologizing for being pastors. Churches grew in numbers and income without any new ideas

1

or programs in evangelism and stewardship. Growth was part of the times.

"In the 1960s, most pastors felt the social scene, with the civil rights battle and the student protests, called for a different way of approaching ministry. For many, the model of the pastor changed. You had people like Martin Luther King, Jr., and leading clergymen in practically every denomination saying that the outstanding role of the church was the prophetic role. The function of the minister, they said, was to stand against the structures of society and to demolish some of them.

"This led to some polarization in the church as to what pastoral ministry was. The pastors who held to a more traditional view felt they had to be apologetic about it because of the aggressiveness of the social-activist pastors, pushed, in part, by the times. And there began to be a great uneasiness in most pastors as to what it was to be a pastor."

Crumley said that if a pastor took a position on any of the great social issues, he would find as many people disagreeing with him as agreeing with him.

"You couldn't preach a sermon that was relevant to the times at all and find a unanimous opinion in the congregation," he recalled. "You would have people waiting after the service to take issue with you as well as people saying, 'Pastor, that was a great sermon.'"

Crumley remembered a sermon he preached when he was pastor of a church in Savannah, Georgia, the Sunday after Martin Luther King, Jr., was assassinated and the "fantastically different reactions" he received from his congregation about the sermon.

Pastors in the 1960s, he noted, were judged not only by their people but by their fellow clergy as to how they handled the controversial issues.

"I think a large segment of society felt that the church failed in the 1960s. Some felt it failed because it had taken too active a position, and others that it hadn't been active enough and its prophetic voice not strong enough. It was one of those situations in which the parish ministry couldn't win.

"In the 1970s," Crumley said, "the apathy that hit society also hit the church. Along with that there were some new factors. A partial carry-over from the 1960s was the strong antiinstitutional bent reflected in the disillusionment with government after Watergate and with technology because of what it had done to the environment. There was a feeling that we were practically brought to bay by forces that were greater than we could handle.

"In the midst of all that, parish ministry had to take on some different connotations. Most pastors felt there had to be some word of comfort, some word of promise, some word of hope. For many pastors, this priestly function became paramount. You couldn't reach out to society or to the world around you because there was a distrust of you simply because you represented an institution—the church."

In recent years there has come a new emphasis on professionalism in the ministry, Crumley said. By this "we have meant more than that you have to be well-trained and effective—you also have a right to plan out what your life will be, what your career will be. At many points this professionalism almost cuts clear across the older idea of calling.

"The idea of professionalism also meant that higher expectations were set for pastors by congregations. We even got into such things as performance evaluations, and pastors knew that at least once during a year with the synod president and council there would likely be a series of questions about how they saw their ministry, where their ministries had moved the past year, and the goals they had for the year ahead."

Dr. Jacob A. O. Preus, president of the Lutheran Church—Missouri Synod (LCMS), said that the most significant feature of society that pastoral ministry has had to deal with since World War II has been its mobility.

The uprooting of people, he noted, has affected churches as it has depleted populations in certain states and resulted in the development of whole new cities, especially in suburbia.

In the process, church members who were caught up in the population movement often were lost to the church. As a result, all of the main-line denominations have suffered what are called back-door losses, he said.

The LCMS president recalled that in his first parish, which he served in the middle of World War II, he was just beginning to experience what it was like to minister to an influx of rural people moving into the city.

The pastor, he said, was kept extremely busy calling on the transplanted Lutherans, many of whom had not yet affiliated with a church.

The unsettledness which resulted from the uprooting brought with it the breakup of many families, Jacob Preus said, citing divorce cases and domestic-relations problems.

As a young parish pastor then, he said he was "totally unequipped to deal with this. I had nothing except what I learned in a textbook on pastoral theology that maybe was written in 1920."

He said the unsettledness had continued with the Korean and Vietnam Wars and later with changes in the economy. The latter, he predicted, may reverse the flow of people from the inner city to the suburbs.

All the changes have meant that the average pastor is often dealing with almost a transient congregation, with the urban pastor—especially the inner-city pastor—finding a totally different world from the rural pastor, he said.

The old ideal of a settled community where everybody lives where they were born, and goes to church and is buried in the church where they were baptized, is a situation which only a minority of Lutherans experience now, Jacob Preus noted.

The LCMS president said he agreed with the view that pastors have lost status in the eyes of society and attributed it partly to the fact that the educational level of the laity no longer contrasts so sharply to that of the pastor.

"He is no longer 'Herr Pastor,'" he observed.

In the Lutheran Church—Missouri Synod, "there has been a gradual and almost imperceptible downgrading of the pastoral office," Jacob Preus told the synod's 1979 convention. He blamed this on the doctrinal controversy that had gone on in the synod for many years. He explained that during the controversy "many people talked about firing their pastors" and they "played kind of fast and loose with calls." There was "a constant harassment" of some pastors.

Jacob Preus said he was happy with the way the synod and its pastors had weathered involvement in social problems during the past three decades. He credited the synod's board of social ministry and synod executives with "not trying to lead us in directions which this conservative, Midwest church would refuse to go." At the same time, he said, the LCMS had succeeded in building a partnership with blacks and Hispanics that did not require them to "burn down buildings" to gain the synod's attention.

Dr. David W. Preus, president of the American Lutheran Church (ALC), said that the biggest change in pastoral ministry he had observed since World War II was the way it had broadened its scope of activities.

"The expectations of the pastor are much more inclusive," he said.

Generally speaking, he said, the focus before World War II was on preaching, teaching, and the availability of the pastor to lead in services, weddings, funerals, and special occasions. Since World War II, he said, there has been a great expansion in the expectations parishioners have for their pastors, such as counseling, community leadership, and organizing a variety of activities, educational opportunities, and missions for the congregation.

The ALC president agreed that increased mobility has had great impact on the church and its ministry. "Things don't stay the same," he noted. "Frequently those who come together in church are strangers rather than persons who have already worshiped together, rejoiced together, and mourned together."

Television also has had a tremendous effect on the church and its ministry, David Preus pointed out. "People feel like they are not being dealt with adequately if they are not being entertained as part of their congregational life," he said.

At the same time, he said, the heightened awareness of critical issues facing the whole human race has required the church to busy itself and the pastor to provide opportunities for congregation members to discover more about such things as nuclear energy, environmental concerns, and other matters.

Asked what directions he expects parish ministry to be taking in the near future, David Preus said: "There has to be a renewed emphasis on the congregation as a supportive and extended family in a mobile society where people are no longer rooted in a single community. We will increasingly see pastors concentrating on interpersonal relationships within the congregation as a family."

The ALC president said he also sees an increasing teaching role for the pastor, "who will function as a kind of principal of a congregation school providing opportunities for people to wrestle with the hard ethical issues facing the church and society.

"There is no way," he observed, "to expect the pastor to be an expert on such issues involving life and death, nuclear weapons, and South Africa, but he can facilitate the learning of his parishioners as they strive to find answers to these difficult questions."

This doesn't mean that congregations are going to try to solve society's problems, he added, but there are particular issues that can only be decided on religious premises.

But the ALC leader emphasized that congregations must not become so concerned with everything else that they lose sight of their fundamental purpose—"to proclaim the gospel of Jesus Christ."

He predicted that there will be "a strengthened local-level, practical ecumenicity—that the local pastor and people are going to have more and more positive cooperative relationships with other Christians—across denominational lines."

And, David Preus emphasized, "it is even more important that the pastor be an everlasting learner. He will have to work at his continuing education because of the rapidity of change."

Jacob Preus said he looks for pastoral ministry to continue to have to deal in the future with the "unsettledness" and mobility of society.

"I think the average pastor will have to develop a great deal of expertise in dealing with children from broken homes, single-parent homes, and no-parent homes," he said. "Things like day-care centers will increase. Ministries to uprooted, uncertain, and confused people, and interracial and multiracial ministries will increase." The LCMS president sees a "tremendous need" to prepare workers to minister to black people, Hispanics, and "all kinds of people at variance from the norm, like homosexuals and drug addicts.

"I think the average pastor is going to have to acquaint himself with law enforcement agencies, education and other government agencies which in some way or the other are trying to cope with the mounting problems of our society," he said.

Jacob Preus said he does not expect ministry in the 1980s to be "a bit easier" than it was in the 1960s, 1950s, or 1940s.

Crumley said ministers should be prepared to serve in a society where there are limitations, such as in energy, and to serve people fearful and anxious about the feeling that society will not be able to solve its problems.

He said the ministry will have to be prepared to deal with "a colossal egocentricity" and "a fantastic 'me' emphasis which advertises that 'you owe it to yourself.'"

Also, he said, ministers will have to have a flexible ministry to deal with families and with congregations made up of widely divergent groups. Congregations will have large contingents of elderly people and probably not as many children, he said. There will be far more singles, he predicted.

In all this he expects the priestly role of the ministry to be very important.

"The church," he said, "must continue to point out in these rapid changes the fact that there are some values that are external—some things we can hold on to—and that there is hope for the future. Along with that, the ministry is going to have to continue to play a strong prophetic role, because limitations in society will make human justice even more difficult to mete out properly."

There may be a demand for more totalitarianism, he said. In order to make things go around, global culture is likely to become less democratic rather than more, he added.

Crumley said the "egocentric" approach of society will make a servant ministry difficult yet more than ever needed. That ministry is going to have to stand over against the threat in culture and call the church to be a servant church, he said.

"The ministry is going to have to develop a strong integrity of its own. We are going to have to know why we want to be ministers, and we are going to have to have a stronger sense of value than ministers previously had."

The LCA president said he believes there will be few places where ministers will be called to build large church buildings. Besides the increasing cost to build and maintain them, Crumley expects congregations to question whether their money might not be used better in other ways.

Crumley said he believes that Americans who have been anti-institutional will look to the church again for answers to their questions when they begin to raise families.

But he said their approach to the church will be different because "they are going to ask the 'God questions' rather than the 'institution questions.'"

This means, he said, that churches will have to become communities of faith—distinctive nurturing and caring communities.

He said ministry in the future will be exciting because it will address itself to the basic questions of existence, to the primary relationship of the person with God and with others.

"The fact that you may not have the resources to go after every new program under the sun may be the best thing that has happened to the church," he said.

Asked which pastoral functions will be important in the near future, Crumley cited the nurturing aspect of the congregation.

"There has to be a concern for bonding people together in the congregation," he said. "If we do this right, it may be the only place most people have bonds."

Besides this pastoral function of caring, Crumley sees a new priority needed on teaching. The "right kind of preaching also will be quite important," he said.

Developing a worshiping community will be important, he said, adding: "I think it is only from that that there can be outreach or social action. You have to start out from a strong home base."

Crumley also sees a need to reach all kinds of people, because "congregations in the future just can't be ethnic conclaves."

David Preus said he believes preaching is going to be more important in the future than it is now. "People are so bombarded with words that quality pulpit efforts are going to be required to claim the attention of parishioners," he said. He noted that the Christian church "simply cannot live and breathe without preaching of the word, but it is going to have to become good preaching."

Thus, the ALC leader pointed out, "after a period of broadening out the scope of the pastor's responsibility now we are going to see an increased awareness of the necessity of making the preaching ministry central and giving it a greater importance than it has had in the past generation."

Jacob Preus also sees preaching and proclaiming the gospel as the center of ministry in the future, but he said the pastor will have to be able to take people "where they are." He will have to be able to listen to them and be an expediter who can help them with their needs and reach out to those who have lost hope. "A very strong emphasis" will be needed on evangelism and outreach, he said.

"The preparation of pastors is going to have to concentrate very, very strongly on equipping ministers and preparing them to relate effectively with people.

"You can't just mount that pulpit, preach a sermon, and vanish into your parsonage and study for the rest of the week," he declared. "It's going to have to be a very people-oriented ministry."

He said personality tests and other analysis will become increasingly important in selecting and preparing candidates for the ministry.

All three church-body presidents talked optimistically about the future and keeping the demand and supply of ministerial candidates in some kind of balance.

The LCMS in mid-1979 had about five hundred parishes with-

out ministers, but every one of them still had the preaching of
the word and administration of the sacraments, mostly because
of the ministry of retired clergy or, in a few cases, through use
of laity and teachers.

Jacob Preus said the LCMS thrives best with about four hundred vacant parishes in order to permit movement of pastors.
He said the synod has had a few "tent-making" ministries in
which the clergy earn their salary at secular occupations while
serving churches. He said he does not expect their number to
increase greatly, observing that they are "hard to handle."

David Preus said the ALC sees itself meeting its clergy needs
adequately. "If anything, it would tilt a little bit on the strong
side," he said. He said the ALC has a sizable number of tent-
making pastors—"farmers, electricians, teachers, and business
people who also serve parishes." He expects a modest increase
in their number but said there is only a limited number of congregations which can use them.

David Preus said the ALC will have a rapid increase in the
number of women entering the parish ministry in the next few
years because of the growing proportion of women (20 to 30
percent) in ALC seminary student bodies. So far, he said, there
has been no effect on the ministry in having women as ministers.
"They do the same things men do and they do them com-
parably," he said.

Crumley said he believes it is inevitable that tent-making
ministries will grow in the LCA. One reason, he explained, is
that the church "always has need to develop creative ministries
but sometimes cannot afford to pay for them. He said it is important that these tent-making ministries be church ministries
"and not just having a person decide what he or she wants
to do."

There are projections that the LCA will have a full supply
of pastors in the years ahead, but he said it is impossible to get
an accurate reading of the situation because of the increasing
numbers of team ministries, women ministers taking maternity
leaves, and declining college enrollments. He said the LCA's big
problem is the lack of mobility for ministers seeking their second
and third calls. There is little movement there, he reported.

Crumley said the LCA's experience with women ministers "had been very positive." In 1979, about one hundred of the LCA's eight thousand ministers were women, and women made up about a fourth of the LCA seminaries' enrollments.

With more women, the complexion of the LCA ministry will change, but Crumley said he was not sure that the church's theology and preaching would be different.

Like the other church presidents, Crumley said a big priority for his church is to build up a support system for its ministers. He believes congregations should help pastors develop confidence in the integrity of what they are doing.

But Crumley cautions congregations against expecting their ministers to know everything and to do everything.

In this connection he recalled his experience as pastor of a congregation in the scientific community of Oak Ridge, Tennessee, which had fifty Ph.D.'s among its three hundred baptized members.

"I tried to stay with them in showing my education and erudition," he recalled. "One of the scientists took me aside and said, 'Pastor, I just feel you are scared.'

"I said, 'Oh yes.'

"He said, 'Just remember we need your field as much as society needs ours, and we are not experts in your field any more than you are an expert in ours.'"

Crumley said the conversation "gave me a sense of being needed, and what I had to do was develop my skills in the things I was supposed to be doing. I didn't have to try to be everything, and that was a terrific help."

One of the most common complaints from clergy is that there are too many things expected of them. One of the more significant things to emerge from the Growth in Ministry Project was that pastors intuitively tend to cluster their various tasks into just six basic roles. In this chapter Marvin Johnson shares these six roles and the tasks that make them up. Then he adds his own thought-provoking implications. He rightly isn't satisfied with just listing the six roles. He wants to challenge us to do something about organizing our ministries around these roles. But there may be a danger hidden in this chapter for pastors more interested in staying popular with their congregations than in leading them. One could concentrate on certain roles like priest and preacher and keep the congregation happy, and ignore others like community and social involvement. But hopefully these pastors are in the minority. Most pastors, though, ought to be able to use these insights to organize their ministries and not to avoid certain less popular aspects.—*Editor*

2

Roles in Pastoring

MARVIN JOHNSON

Pastors sometimes feel pulled in many different directions by the pressure of time and the almost endless list of activities they are expected to perform. What if these activities could be organized and reduced to six basic roles? There are at least two advantages of thinking about six roles instead of dozens of activities. It assists pastors to gain control of their time and life, and to provide a more balanced ministry.

The six roles were actually determined by the Growth in Ministry participants themselves. By a process called factor analysis, their responses to certain sets of questions clustered themselves into the six groupings we call pastoral roles.

Several years ago Fred Kling, a Presbyterian minister, analyzed statements about ministry by clergy from six major Protestant denominations. The thirty activities he developed were the backbone of this more recent study. They include (not in order of priorities):

1. Maps out objectives and plans the overall church strategy and program
2. Teaches and works directly with children
3. Leads public worship
4. Ministers to the sick, dying, and bereaved
5. Counsels with people facing the major decisions of life—marriage, vocations
6. Fosters fellowship at church gatherings
7. Teaches and works directly with young people
8. Talks with individuals about their spiritual development
9. Visits new residents and recruits new members
10. Supplies ideas for new activities and projects

13

11. Works with congregational boards and committees
12. Recruits, trains, and assists lay leaders and teachers
13. Manages the church office—records, correspondence, information center
14. Preaches sermons
15. Follows a definite schedule of reading and study
16. Promotes and creates enthusiasm for church activities
17. Maintains a disciplined life of prayer and personal devotion
18. Cooperates with social, legal, medical, and educational workers
19. Helps manage church finances
20. Administers baptism and communion; conducts weddings and sacred rites
21. Participates in denominational activities
22. Teaches and works directly with adults
23. Counsels with people about their moral and personal problems
24. Cultivates his or her home and personal life
25. Participates in community projects and organizations
26. Mixes socially to develop contacts
27. Maintains harmony, handles troublemakers, averts or resolves problems
28. Assists victims of social neglect or injustice
29. Speaks to community and civic groups
30. Visits regularly in the homes of the congregation

When the associations between these thirty activities were discovered, the six groupings, or roles, were given names based on their contents. The six roles are:

I. Priest and Preacher
II. Spiritual and Personal Development
III. Organizer
IV. Teacher-Visitor
V. Office Administrator
VI. Community and Social Involvement

Some of these roles are predictable, but others hold some surprises—those serendipities which can make for useful insights and implications. It is worth noting that item 22, "Teaches and works directly with adults," did not belong to any one role but figured to some degree in every role.

In the following pages the six roles will be described one at a time with a brief mention of possible implications. These implications are suggestive, not exhaustive.

The discussion of these roles is intended not to produce guilt but to increase work freedom, that is, to suggest ways of viewing ministry as a wholistic impact of six basic roles which cover just about any conceivable pastoral activity.

THE PRIEST AND PREACHER ROLE

Item Number	Items
4	Ministers to the sick, dying, and bereaved
14	Preaches sermons
3	Leads public worship
20	Administers baptism and communion; conducts weddings and sacred rites
5	Counsels with people facing the major decisions of life—marriage, vocations

Of the thirty activities, only five are clustered into the *priest and preacher* role. In the chart above, the items are listed according to their closeness to the essence of the role. In other words, item 4 is closer to what it means to be a priest and preacher than item 5. Yet item 5 is important nonetheless.

The priest and preacher role has top priority among pastors and laity because people want a word and sacrament ministry. A young man who had attended church as a child but has since dropped out looked at the priest and preacher role and said, "I am not surprised, those are the things people expect a pastor to do." He is right. People expect their pastor to lead public worship; preach; conduct sacraments and rites; and counsel with the sick, dying, bereaved, and those facing major decisions in life. People want a pastor who gets involved when they need and want the pastor. Those who enjoy the word and sacrament ministry are probably in the right profession. But pastors who enjoy some but not all of these activities should consider new ways to enjoy the troublesome ones. Pastors who dislike the activities of word and sacrament ministry may, frankly, be in the wrong profession.

The priest and preacher role is the key to an effective and fulfilling ministry. If this role is second or third in the priority list, the pastor is probably out of phase with the congregation and with original purposes for entering the ministry.

If a pastor is effective in the priest and preacher role, the laity will be happy and tend to overlook or accept some deficiencies in the other roles. No pastor can do a perfect job in every role. There is always room to improve. It is essential for pastors to be effective in the priest and preacher role. But who decides effectiveness? The people. If people think pastors are effective, they are effective, even though they know where they can and ought to improve, and even if they think some of their peers are more effective. People may be able to live with a pastor who is not an outstanding preacher if he or she is solid in other elements of the priest and preacher role, for example, conducting public worship, visiting the sick, dying, and bereaved, and so forth. Church members tend to look at their pastors wholistically in terms of roles, not in terms of specific activities.

Pastors who are not good at certain of the priest and preacher activities probably can do something about that. These pastors should isolate those obstacles which deaden their effectiveness. Could it be attitude, or a lack of skill, or an inadequate education? There are ways to adjust any of these situations.

Those who make the priest and preacher role the top priority will discover more work freedom and sanity in their busy schedules.

Most pastors suffer from time pressure, and many feel guilty about all the things which are left undone. They find it difficult, for instance, to take time for themselves and their families. Spending adequate time and energy, though, doing those things con-

16

sidered most important, makes it easier to postpone some things or handle criticisms about what has not been done. Everyone knows the pastor can't do it all. But those who fail to work at the priest and preacher role will get criticism.

Pastors who do not like to visit the sick, dying, and bereaved, and avoid those visits for whatever reasons, will be in constant trouble with their parishioners. Loneliness and anxieties can be overwhelming, and a pastoral visit really does matter. Pastors who have difficulty with sick and shut-in or bereavement calls should set some goals for change. This is an important part of the call to a parish, and pastors and the people are aware of that.

The impression given in the pulpit and in public worship is also crucial to the priest and preacher role. Many people have no contact with their pastor at any other time. They decide on that brief contact if the pastor is a person who lives the gospel and can help them to live the gospel in their daily lives, particularly when they are faced with sickness, death, or major problems.

It is important for pastors to discover what kind of impression they give in public. Trusted and honest members can be very helpful here if they share positive *and* negative feedback. Audio tapes and especially videotapes can offer real revelations.

When pastors counsel people about their major decisions or about moral and personal problems, they are performing not a counseling *role* but a counseling *function* which is a part of the priest and preacher role.

People probably do not see their clergy as counselors, but as pastors who are able to counsel with them about their problems and needs. They are likely to come to a pastor for counseling if the pastor is a faithful priest and preacher who has sent out signals in preaching and visiting which say, "I can accept you as you are and will help you to grow if you want to grow."

Historically, the tasks in the priest and preacher role have been the "stuff" of the Christian ministry. Clergy and lay people have reconfirmed that they still consider this to be so. This is the role that separates the ministry from other people-oriented organizations. The other five roles are also important, but the nature of a pastor's ministry is shaped by his or her acceptance of *this* role. Its importance cannot be overestimated.

THE SPIRITUAL AND PERSONAL GROWTH ROLE

Item Number	Items
17	Maintains a disciplined life of prayer and personal devotion
15	Follows a definite schedule of reading and study
24	Cultivates his or her home and personal life
23	Counsels with people about their moral and personal problems

People expect pastors to be spiritual persons, persons they can model themselves after, who wrestle with the issues of life in terms of faith. They also expect pastors to have a spiritual discipline, probably a definite time and place each day, for prayer and personal devotion. They expect a definite schedule for reading and study.

Finally, people expect their pastors to have an integrated personal, spiritual, and family life.

Research shows that whereas pastors and laity agree that the pastor's spiritual and personal growth is very important, the pastors admit that in reality their spiritual and personal growth is not as good as the lay people imagine it to be. Why? Is it modesty on the pastor's part or is it admission that something is wrong?

For those interested in improving their spiritual life, the *spiritual and personal development* role offers clues to a working definition of what is needed to clear away those things which impede a relationship with Christ and the work of the Holy Spirit.

Set aside a definite time and place each day, a unique discipline, for prayer and personal devotion. It is easy to use time as an excuse. How often have pastors said, "I don't have time for prayer and personal devotion"? Many subscribe to the pray-as-you-work or pray-as-you-run idea. Often what these really amount to is a way to avoid prayer and a way to stunt spiritual growth.

Follow a definite schedule of reading and study too. No matter how busy pastors are, they are like everyone else. Clergy actually spend their time doing pretty much what they want to do! If that is difficult to believe, just look back over the last week of 168 hours. How much was spent on what you wanted to do?

Pastors should strive to correlate their family, personal, and spiritual lives. Those who try to live family, personal, and spiritual lives separately from one another often discover that all of these become poverty-stricken. Pastors who find it painful to share their spiritual life with their spouse or friends may find that that very pain is the subject matter which, if explored, will enrich both their own spiritual life and their life with spouse and friends. Correlating family life, personal life, and spiritual life means integrating them. It is not an accident that the words *integrate* and *integrity* come from the same Latin root meaning "to make whole, to renew."

The ability to counsel with people about their moral and personal problems grows out of being an authentic pastor, a person of God. The pastor's own spiritual life does affect the helping relationship between the pastor and the people.

The late Sidney Jourard pioneered in the self-disclosure model of counseling. He found that the degree to which the counselee is able to reveal himself or herself to the counselor is directly proportional to the self-disclosure of the counselor. In other words, if a counselor can reveal struggles, doubts, and breakthroughs, the counselees can do the same. If, however, a pastor's spiritual development is arrested, how will he or she assist the person who comes for help?

Congregations expect their pastors to get things organized; to be the person with intention and a sense of direction. This is a big order. It depends on leadership style. Pastors may be autocratic or democratic, but they must lead. They cannot remain laissez-faire and wait for the people to get organized. Let's face it, pastors get paid to do the job, and part of the job is the role of *organizer*.

THE ORGANIZER ROLE

Item Number	Items
10	Supplies ideas for new activities and projects
12	Recruits, trains, and assists lay leaders and teachers
11	Works with congregational boards and committees
1	Maps out objectives and plans the overall church strategy and program
16	Promotes and creates enthusiasm for church activities
27	Maintains harmony, handles troublemakers, averts or resolves problems

The organizer role is important, because people want to belong to an organization which gets things done. When a congregation is disorganized and lacks direction, people will get discouraged and even drop out. One pastor eventually drove away the best talent in the congregation. The pastor supplied plenty of ideas, was enthusiastic, and had clear objectives and plans. He was able to recruit people to become involved. His problem was that he didn't really think other people could do things as well as he could. He would not delegate and let people carry out the plans. He did it all himself. Many ideas never saw the light of day. The congregation was basically disorganized. The best leaders left. The less competent leaders followed the pastor. The irony of it all was that the pastor never figured out what was the root of his problem. When he was sixty-five years old the congregation forced him to retire. They had had enough.

The organizer role is one of the clearest opportunities for creativity in ministry. Each of the six pastoral roles gives opportunity for creativity, but the organizer role focuses clearly on creativity. This is particularly noted in item 10, "supplies ideas for new activities and projects."

People expect the pastor to be a planner, but the research

showed that many pastors are not planners. They wake up in the morning and let the day happen to them. They do not plan their day and do not assume the organizer role for their parish. Their excuse for this lack of planning is that contingencies will happen and thwart their plans anyway. Surely contingencies happen, but not every day.

Those who hate administration may be avoiding the role which can give them and their congregations a unique sense of mission, that is, the unique role of *this* pastor in *this* congregation in *this* context at *this* time.

Everyone can be a better organizer. Some people will never be super organizers, but being the organizer does not mean that they must do it all themselves. People in the congregation can help. Pastors and laity can cooperate to make the best of the organizer role.

Even Moses, the man who led thousands out of Egypt, needed advice and help as an organizer. In Genesis 18, Jethro saw how Moses was wearing himself and the people out with poor organization. Jethro showed Moses how to delegate tasks and responsibilities, and things were simplified immediately.

The congregation expects its pastor to maintain harmony, handle troublemakers, and avert and resolve problems as a part of the organizer role. Conflict is normal. People (especially pastors) easily forget that fact. Whenever two or more people work together there will be conflicts. How conflicts are handled is crucial to the organizer role. Ignoring conflict and hoping it will go away is not conflict resolution. Conflict resolution is a process of identifying the conflict, dealing with the conflict, and working out an amicable solution.

Finally, the organizer role discloses that pastors are expected to promote and create enthusiasm for church activities. Enthusiasm literally means "to be filled with the Spirit of God." A basically quiet, introverted pastor was hard to get to know. But he had what might be called "quiet enthusiasm." He believed in what the congregation was doing. No one doubted his enthusiasm. Pastors do not have to change their personalities to be enthusiastic. But if the organizer is not enthusiastic, he or she should not expect the people to be enthusiastic.

THE TEACHER AND VISITOR ROLE

Item Number	*Items*
7	Teaches and works directly with young people
2	Teaches and works directly with children
30	Visits regularly in the homes of the congregation
8	Talks with individuals about their spiritual development

The first thing one pastor said to a synod convention after being elected president was "Now I won't have to teach that confirmation class again." Many pastors like to teach adults but hate to teach children and youth. Most pastors, the research showed, think teaching is important but do not know if they are effective or not! Does that hit home? If so, there is probably a good reason. Some pastors simply do not know how to teach! Maybe they were never taught how to teach children, and what they do know, they learned by trial and error. What can be done about it? There are resources in every community: seminars, workshops, books, and people. One person who can help is the successful junior high school teacher. The kids know who that person is. Ask them.

Perhaps there is guilt and frustration about the *teacher-visitor* role because both activities consume large blocks of time and it is difficult to see immediate results. One major reason why teaching and/or visiting is guilt-producing and frustrating for so many pastors is that their goals are too ambitious and not precisely focused. Pastors have to struggle to set realistic and attainable goals which meet the students where they are, instead of where the pastor thinks they *ought* to be. Many other frustrated pastors simply need to set less ambitious goals for their teaching and visiting. For example, is it realistic to try to visit a hundred households in a year? How many visits is that per week? Two households per week is likely a realistic goal. But what happens if the goal is two hundred to three hundred households in a year? What is realistic? Pastors who set realistic goals which their church officers can buy into find a healthy reduction of guilt and frustration. Why not feel good instead of bad?

When planning visits in the homes of members, pastors might focus the visits on spiritual development. Henry Melchior Muhlenberg, the colonial pastor, reported on many home visits in his journals. Sometimes it might take him as much as two or three days on horseback to arrive at the home he had chosen. After the usual passing of the time of day he regularly reported that he and the family had an "edifying discourse." Muhlenberg focused his visits on spiritual development. He was combining the teaching and visiting activity into a teacher-visitor role. The result was a building up of the saints.

In a visit in a person's home the pastor is perceived to be a teacher, one who knows, one who can answer questions or help with problems or needs. How a visit is handled can make it useful or a waste of time. So often it happens that as the pastor visits in a home, someone says, "Pastor, I have always wanted to ask you about . . ." or "Pastor, what do you think about . . . ?" The pastor is a "presence," a person who embodies to people the presence of God, the presence of the church, or that certain something called "a person of God." Home visits can become a great opportunity to help persons. Or they can be a waste of time.

THE OFFICE ADMINISTRATOR ROLE

Item Number	Items
19	Helps manage church finances
13	Manages the church office—records, correspondence, information center
9	Visits new residents and recruits new members

Pastors are responsible for enough office administration so that the congregation has an adequate system for handling finances, records, and correspondence and so that the office is an adequate center for information. Pastors do not need to do all the office administration themselves but are held accountable for a smooth operation. Many spend too much time in the office because they like that work better than those roles which take them out to meet people.

Some pastors and leaders tend to think of visiting new residents and recruiting new members as being related to managing finances and office management. No doubt the idea has crossed every pastor's mind that "if we get more new members we will have bigger weekly offerings."

For a number of years I was involved in recruiting persons for an organization. That organization emphasized the idea of "hovering close to new people" for the first few months. New people have a need for information about how the organization works and how they fit in. They need coaching. Certain members of the group work closely with new members to keep them informed. Many of the new people do not wait to be informed at formal meetings; they get on the phone and talk to someone who can answer questions. New members of any organization, including the church, need an information center—a place that knows. And they need contact with people who care.

The congregation expects that new residents and new members will be visited whether the pastor personally makes the calls or not. A pastor of a mission congregation was frustrated and felt guilty about the calls he made on new members. He also had an evangelism committee who made calls. They decided to keep records and gather data. A year later, when they analyzed their data, they decided to modify their strategy because they discovered that they got the best results if two lay persons made the initial calls on new residents and the pastor only called on those people who the team thought were likely prospects.

Pastors are seen by their congregations as a liaison between the community and the congregation. The liaison function includes two types of activities: service to people in the community and involvement in activities which benefit the congregation. The pastor is a public person, and what he or she says and does is noticed by a surprising number of people.

THE COMMUNITY AND SOCIAL INVOLVEMENT ROLE

Item Number	*Items*
29	Speaks to community and civic groups
25	Participates in community projects and organizations
26	Mixes socially to develop contacts
18	Cooperates with social, legal, medical, and educational workers
28	Assists victims of social neglect or injustice
21	Participates in denominational activities
6	Fosters fellowship at church gatherings

The pastor who thinks that the *community and social involvement* role is more important than his or her lay leaders think it is, though, is probably inviting trouble. But the reverse is true too. A pastor who could not care less about community and social involvement is probably in for trouble with lay leaders for not fulfilling their expectation as a "presence" in the community.

A LAST WORD TO PASTORS

Before you finish this chapter, think about a goal for your ministry in each of the pastoral roles and jot these goals down on paper. As you think about the next year in your parish, which of the six roles need major influence?

Now, imagine yourself planning the next week around each of the six roles. What is already on your calendar? How do those things fit the roles? Which role is getting the most emphasis?

Try on the six roles as you would a new pair of shoes. See if they "feel right" as a way of carrying out ministry for the next months, and test them in the reality of your situation.

Talking about shared ministry is somewhat like talking about motherhood and apple pie. No one is going to speak against a ministry which is shared between the congregation and the pastor. But for all this, far too many congregations and pastors complain that they can't get help from each other. Joe Wagner offers us some views about what shared ministry is and how it differs from other models. He challenges us to consider our own ministries and how they can grow as cooperative efforts between the pastor and the congregation. But he warns that adjusting a ministry to become a shared effort is not easy. In many congregations long patterns have been established, and they don't die easily. Is it worth the effort? Each reader will have to decide. Pessimists will no doubt conclude that this chapter will make few converts. Too many pastors will have to step down from their pedestal and accept some hard and potentially frustrating work. But the optimists among us may argue that most pastors are looking for the kinds of suggestions that Pastor Wagner offers here.—*Editor*

3

Shared Ministry

JOSEPH WAGNER

Shared ministry is no mysterious thing. It has elements which can be identified, understood, and worked for. It can be defined as "pastor and people holding mutual values and working together to achieve commonly held ministry goals."

One of the first things that many pastors discover upon accepting a new call is that the way ministry works in one place may bear little resemblance to the way it worked in the other. In one congregation, the ministry flowed naturally. The feelings between pastor and people seemed amiable, and the ministry was accomplished in a general atmosphere of mutual support; while in the other, the chemistry is not quite right. Pastor and people are at different places, and ministering together is a chore—a series of starts, stops, and hesitations.

While a number of different factors certainly play into these two experiences, a key element which is present in the first and absent in the second is a sense of shared ministry between the pastor and the people.

There are certain marks to look for in congregations which are involved in a shared ministry. One apparent characteristic is a laity which feels some "ownership" of the ministry happening there. This may be represented by a group of creative lay people who share in the pastor's struggle to prepare a meaningful Lenten program. This is in marked contrast to another congregation where the pastor plans, produces, and hands the Lenten program to the people.

Ownership extends to other aspects of ministry, too. When the

27

laity feel responsible for the ministry, they may, for instance, give greater energies to recruiting and training evangelism visitors rather than just sitting back and blaming the pastor for the lagging membership.

But shared ministry goes beyond the simple *doing* of ministry together. It also involves *how* that ministry is done. The same evangelism committee chairperson who has assembled the troops to work on the lagging membership may be consumed by her fears of returning home to a marriage which is troubled. She is both congregational leader and worried wife. How the pastor and committee work with her may say much about their feeling of shared ministry. In a like manner, the laity ministers to the pastor who is not only a leader but also one who has private concerns and fears. Shared ministry means a pastor and people ministering to one another as well as together serving the needs of others.

It can happen anywhere, too. The congregation may be large or small, simple or complex, urban or rural. The key is that at its heart that congregation shares a clear sense of what is going on. The pastor and people are open and honest about how they see their work together in the tasks and interpersonal relationships of their ministry. In short, they've braved a look at how they provide or deny support to one another.

Even though the marks of a shared ministry may be easy to identify, achieving it is not easy. It involves commitment to this style of ministry by both congregation and pastor. It assumes that both parties are willing and able to be honest with each other in expressing their ideas and feelings. It involves a process for understanding the mutual expectations which each has of the other and a way of presenting these expectations. Finally, shared ministry implies a continuing process of evaluating, checking signals, and planning for the future. Our Lord once admonished his followers to bear one another's burdens. Shared ministry is a style of congregational ministry based upon that theme.

As there are observable marks of a congregation involved in a shared ministry, there are also marks of those which are not. The following examples illustrate some of those kinds of separate ministries.

THE IDLING CONGREGATION

Pastor Smith is serving a congregation of four hundred baptized members with Sunday attendance of about two hundred. He is working as hard as he feels he can, fifty to sixty hours per week, but still things hardly ever seem to be going quite the way he would like. He was told when he came that the congregation "had potential," and he believed it. Located on the growing edge of a medium-sized town, St. James Church still seems to him to have potential. But no matter how hard he works, he feels little sense of accomplishment. He knows that he is being faithful to his Lord, but words of encouragement are slow in coming from the congregation. Furthermore, it seems that there is always so much more to be done. Routine visits in the homes of members do not get made, and advanced planning for coming events slips until the last minute. Sermon preparation time is sliced thinner than it should be as hospital calls, committee meetings, and counseling demand more of his time.

In contrast to his time and effort, it seems congregational members are not very involved. Most committees are barely struggling along and seem unsure of what they should really be doing. The congregation as a whole, though, is not dissatisfied or discouraged with the situation. That, in fact, is part of the problem. They believe that things are going along just fine! They attend worship with some regularity and the pastor is available when they need him.

This situation is not uncommon. Separate ministries exist at St. James with no clear focus for the congregation's or the pastor's work and no helpful way available for analyzing just what is going on. There is no sense of shared ministry. The potential of the congregation is not being realized, yet the pastor is overworked and feeling little satisfaction in what he is doing.

THE "CASUAL FRIENDS" CONGREGATION

St. James is at a crossroads and may not even realize it. The people and Pastor Smith are on the verge of enforcing their separate ministries and adopting a mode of relating to each other which we can call "casual friends." Pastor and congregation exist in a symbiotic relationship—each deriving something from the other but neither really investing itself in the other.

The pastor, tiring of long hours with little encouragement or sense of movement, may begin to do only the most obvious activities and to slight other things. He may devote more time to those things which interest him in his personal life or in community activities, or to looking for another congregation to serve. The zest will have left his efforts.

The congregation may also adjust itself to some lower aspirations, being satisfied with fewer services from the pastor as long as he doesn't make them feel too uncomfortable with their own second-best production. They are "casual friends." To a visitor, the congregation appears complacent, without much ambition, and not interested in changing.

THE "STALEMATE" CONGREGATION

If St. James were a bit more intense or if it had stronger lay leadership, it might find itself operating in the "stalemate" mode. In this situation the congregation, believing itself to have potential, is willing to move in the direction of shared ministry with Pastor Smith. But the pastor, though overworked, is somehow not willing or able to take the risk of really trusting the lay leadership. Lay leadership emerges, assumes positions of responsibility, but then is not allowed to develop strength and momentum. Shortly, the leaders become discouraged, burned out, and decline future leadership opportunities.

The pastor appears to hang back as if afraid the lay members may take over territory which he considers to be his own. Perhaps he is uncertain of what might happen if they were turned loose. And so the congregation misses the opportunity to become a dynamic group and is unable to realize the potential which is latent in its members and its pastor. Stalemate has emerged as an alternative to shared ministry.

What elements in these examples prevent shared ministry from occurring? The problem is not primarily with the level of desire of either pastor or people. Each, at least in the early stages of their life together, wanted more sharing. The opportunity for new beginnings fires the early months of each new pastorate. The problem lay first in the absence of a shared vision for what they might become together, second in not knowing and analyzing the special gifts each brings to the ministry, and third in having no realistic plan for using their gifts to pursue their vision.

St. James could just continue along. It might just idle for several years after Pastor Smith's arrival, waiting for something to happen. Operating as casual friends can even become rather comfortable for all concerned. If there are no intrusions from the outside, it can go on almost indefinitely. The stalemate mode, with its building pressure, will usually come apart more quickly, breaking under the stress of frustrated hopes and unaccomplished plans.

TOWARD SOME SOLUTIONS

The good thing about problems is that contained within them are clues to solutions and real opportunities for growth. Pain is a teacher, and frustration is a strong motivator.

Where might St. James Church go from here? Whether in an idling, casual friends, or stalemate situation, we assume that they can change for the better. Some precipitating event will occur, brought about by sufficient pain or promise. Something will occur to break loose the standoff and provide the opportunity for pastor and congregation to look at some other possibilities.

A new challenge or a new goal may present itself to the congregation. They may experience an influx of families hired by new industry—a new housing development might take shape in the church's neighborhood. The real possibility of expanding the facility might develop. A new challenge might arise to serve the needs of a changing neighborhood. Or the under-the-surface pressure of the stalemated congregation might give rise to a direct confrontation between pastor and people. Such conflict should be dealt with openly and be the occasion for considering more promising options.

Yet another precipitating event might be the recognition of the congregation's gradual sliding from strength toward weakness. This might likely occur in the casual friends setting, in which the congregation and pastor coast without generating new ideas or encouraging fresh growth. Sometimes this recognition is triggered by a more drastic event, such as the pastor's physical or emotional collapse from the stress of attempting so many separated ministries. Whatever the cause, whether pain or promise, the congregation whose ministry style is separate rather than shared does have opportunities to stop, to reexamine, and to begin to change to a shared ministry approach.

THE SHARED MINISTRY STYLE

What does a congregation that is engaged in shared ministry with its pastor look like? There is no ideal typical congregation. Pastors and congregations are too distinctive for that. The specifics of exactly how a pastor and congregation relate to one another are always the result of the day-to-day interchange of the particular congregation. The personality, commitment, and skills of the pastor blend with the corporate point of view, resources, and commitment of the congregation to produce the stage upon which the ministry occurs.

Shared ministry is done almost by intuition in many congregations. But in following intuition, certain important aspects may be overlooked or ignored. Five key elements must mark a responsible approach to this style of pastor-congregation interaction.

Shared Ministry

1. *The pastor and congregation must share a vision for their life together.* This vision may be developed by a thorough study or by a more simple process. Some suggestions for this process are included later in this chapter. Whatever the techniques used to identify them, goals for the congregation's ministry and for the pastor's roles in that common ministry must be understood and agreed upon.

2. *The pastor and people must share a spirit of trust and openness.* This implies a *willingness* to share ideas and feelings and an *openness* to change and growth in relationships and responsibilities.

3. *They must analyze their resources.* This involves knowing the gifts, skills, and degrees of willingness which pastor and people bring to the ministry they share. What are the special strengths of the pastor? What special history, opportunity, and gifts does the congregation bring?

4. *They must develop a plan.* The plan should organize and coordinate the linkup between resources and the tasks of ministry which are to be accomplished. It should be made in such a way that all participants in the ministry have a maximum of room in which to move. All who share in the ministry need to feel a sense of fulfillment within their areas of responsibility or activity.

5. *They must create opportunities for checking signals and identifying accomplishments.* Not only is such evaluation necessary in order to be responsible, but it also creates the opportunity to celebrate accomplishments and to share the hurt of failures.

Can you think yourself back into a setting in which you as pastor or congregational member felt strongly that things were going well between pastor and people? Most of us can do that and can learn from the experience. Why not take a few minutes to do just that? Take a sheet of paper and title it "A Shared Ministry—Personal Reflections."

Now list the following headings, two on the front and three spaced down the back of the sheet, leaving room for your comments:

1. Shared Vision
2. Trust and Openness
3. Analysis of Resources
4. Planning and Doing
5. Evaluation and Recognition

Now think of a specific task or project in which you were involved when pastor and people worked closely and effectively together. Resist the temptation to think of too broad an issue. Restrict your thinking to a particular project or activity that you can recall clearly.

Next, jot down your observations on the sheet. Include the answers to some of these questions in your comments.

1. Shared Vision
   a. What objective were you working on?
   b. In what ways was the objective important to both pastor and congregation?
   c. In what ways was the objective related to strongly held values or to the primary purposes of the church and its mission?
   d. What differing points of view did pastor and people have regarding the objective, and how were these points of view brought together?
   e. What parts of the task belonged primarily to the pastor? What belonged to other participants?

2. Trust and Openness
   a. As you worked together, when were you aware of the feelings of those who were involved?
   b. Were these feelings dealt with? If so, how did that happen?
   c. To what degree did participants feel free to raise objections and to inject different points of view and "better ideas"?
   d. How did the group respond to such divergent opinions?

3. Analysis of Resources
   a. List some special skills which were brought to the task by the pastor.
   b. List some special skills which were brought to the task by others who participated.
   c. What material resources were necessary to accomplish the objective?
   d. On a one-to-ten scale, how would you rate the degree of willingness brought to the task by the various participants?

4. Planning and Doing
   a. What steps or stages were included in the plan to meet the objective?
   b. Was the plan clear to all? Agreed to by all? Realistic? Tied to target dates?
   c. How much freedom did each participant have to pursue his or her assigned responsibilities?
   d. What person or group was responsible for monitoring progress?
   e. How was the task concluded?

5. Evaluation and Recognition
   a. What sort of evaluation was made of the work done to accomplish the objectives?
   b. What learnings carried over into subsequent activities in the congregation?
   c. In what ways were the accomplishments celebrated and the participants given recognition?

How do you feel about this exercise? If you haven't done it yet, promise yourself to set aside thirty minutes in the next two days to do so.

Assuming you have reflected on a real situation, you probably have some new insights into how an actual example of shared ministry works. Were there some blank areas on your sheet that you could not complete? Why did these occur? Was it just a matter of bad memory, or were some important elements omitted from the incident? How hard was it to recall an example? The ease or difficulty you found might indicate the degree to which you are engaged in shared ministry.

Regardless of what observations you might make regarding the state of shared ministry in your congregation now, it is always possible to improve on things. The research on which this book is based indicated, in fact, that pastors and congregations are pretty well pleased with one another. Levels of fulfillment are good, and the typical pastor and congregation are on healthy terms with one another.

So we are working at the somewhat elusive task of stimulating healthy pastors and congregations to become even stronger and more effective. Most of us have a hard time motivating ourselves to become better at doing something we are already doing adequately. It is much easier, for instance, to be motivated to recover from a real failure or to resolve to avoid future problems after a brush with near disaster.

The preceding exercise is related to this issue of motivation. Upon reflection, even a good experience has in it some points for improvement. Perhaps the most important insight from the exercise is that a series of successful individual incidents of shared ministry creates shared ministry on a larger scale.

One good way of establishing a shared ministry is to apply the learnings from small examples to the larger context of the total congregation's work. The rather simple dynamics of a single event are easily understood. The trick is then to translate the experiences of the small example into the larger and more complex matters of comprehensive congregational shared ministry. In more simple cases, moving from step to step by intuition may work well, but it fails when the entire ministry of a congregation and pastor is considered.

Let's look at how a congregation might initiate a shared ministry style.

SHARED VISION

Shared vision becomes intriguingly complex when we seek to analyze and understand the points of view of both congregation and pastor. Unless the pastor and people share an understanding about the fundamental commitments and general focus of the congregation's life, there will be little sense of congregational direction. Congregational life will feel like a series of short-term, repeating cycles without a sense of long-term purpose or progress.

For instance, all congregations understand what comprise the basic ingredients necessary for survival. The church must remain open and the bills must be paid. There must be worship, opportunities for study, and fellowship. Depending upon the size, complexity, and vision of the congregation, other elements are added, such as outreach, service, and nurture. Persons or committees assume responsibility for managing these concerns, which usually include annual and predictable cycles of activities. The stewardship campaign, the recruitment of Sunday school teachers, and worship events related to the festivals of the church year exemplify these cycles. But the question remains, what pulls them all together?

It is the congregation's and pastor's shared vision which integrates their activities. It provides the background for coordinating and monitoring their progress. How is this vision achieved? In most cases, it develops unnoticed over considerable time. The pieces slowly fall together until a pattern emerges and is unconsciously understood and accepted by both pastor and people. The pattern may simply be the composite of all the individual cycles of activities. This crazy quilt of separate pieces does fit together in some way, but it can hardly be considered a real vision or purpose.

A sense of shared vision can be established in a more intentional way and have a much greater likelihood of success. Establishing this shared vision between pastor and people requires two things: (1) understanding the congregation's goals for its life of nurture and outreach and (2) understanding how the pastor participates in these goals.

There are many plans and approaches to congregational goal setting and planning. They range from comprehensive systems requiring a heavy investment of time, talent, and energy to rather superficial approaches which may be accomplished in one or two meetings. The benefits are proportional to the investment. But regardless of the specific approach, goal setting and planning are essential for establishing a shared vision. Goal setting and planning should involve broad congregational participation. All persons should be given opportunities to invest their ideas and efforts in the process.

An element almost always overlooked in congregational goal setting is, surprisingly, the role of the pastor. Often the pastor stands on the sidelines while lay leaders who may do such planning in their work guide the goal setting and planning. Such lay involvement is good, but the pastor has a special and influential position in a congregation's life. He or she occupies a position unique to the church and different from supervisors in other organizations.

Here we refer to the pastoral activities and roles described in chapter 2. The research which undergirds this book provides accurate and usable descriptions of pastoral roles which can be employed in making the essential connection between pastoral activities and congregational goals.

Here's a sketch of just how this can happen. Imagine, for instance, that St. James and Pastor Smith decided that a high priority was to attract prospective members and to integrate them into the fellowship of their congregation. This goal is important because it is consistent with their most fundamental commitment to spread the good news of Jesus Christ. It is also responsive to new growth in the community and the need to strengthen the congregation. Congregational leaders might plan for lay visits to new residents. They intend to express a genuine and friendly acceptance of first-time visitors, to provide continuing contact with prospects, and to quickly integrate new members into the congregation's programs. But attention should also be given to the part the pastor plays in this goal. As priest and preacher, how do his or her personal presence, conduct of the worship service, and preaching contribute to the goal of attracting and integrating new members? In what ways does the pastor as organizer relate to the goal? As organizer, she or he identifies and encourages lay leaders and promotes enthusiasm among members. How might these activities include prospects and new members?

The points of contact between congregation and pastor are legion. Shared vision is clarified and developed in the interface between congregational goals and pastoral roles. Where high-priority congregational goals coincide with highly important pastoral activities, key opportunities for establishing the congregation's vision are born. More about this later.

TRUST AND OPENNESS

Perhaps the most elusive of all the requirements for shared ministry are trust and openness. Without them shared ministry is impossible. We can tell when it is present. Pastor and people know instinctively whether the atmosphere is clear for honest communication. The stalemated congregation described earlier generates dynamics which prevent trust and openness from flourishing. There is so much static and edginess that no one ventures to make real feelings and opinions known.

How can trust and openness be encouraged? Trust does not develop in a vacuum. It happens as people work and share together. As goals are set and pursued, trust and openness are also being developed. As differing opinions and feelings are worked through, patterns of honesty and openness develop. These patterns then seem to multiply themselves into the total network of relationships in the congregation.

The trust between pastor and people is nourished in the intimacies of counseling and crisis visitation, in the manner and content of preaching, and in the attitudes and energy evident as pastor and people share the work of ministry. A consistent willingness for openness and trust is required of both the pastor and the congregation in each of these settings. Trust and openness, essential elements in love, will cover a multitude of sins in the pastor-parish relationship.

ANALYSIS OF RESOURCES

Here we deal with the nuts and bolts of equipment and hardware. In the people business of the church we turn naturally to people resources. Dollars and bricks and mortar are needed, but they are never the heart of the issue. The church is built up first and last of "living stones," the folks who pray, sweat, cry, and celebrate together.

We have talked of congregational goals and of pastoral roles. That is another way of saying people resources. Any responsible plan of action requires an evaluation of resources. Shared ministry means sharing the individual skills, strengths, capacities, insights, faith, and commitment of the participants in ministry. The church is an organization made up almost entirely of volunteers—persons who have abundant skills developed through living and working and who can, if motivated and enabled, blend this pool of resources into effective ministry.

In analyzing your congregation's resources, be sure to look carefully at how the resources of pastor and people cluster around certain key areas of congregational needs and goals. Note especially those intersections between pastoral roles and congregational goals. Here are some key intersections to watch for.

In the congregational area of:	*Note especially the pastor's roles as:*
Worship	Priest and Preacher Teacher and Visitor Personal and Spiritual Growth
Learning	Teacher and Visitor Personal and Spiritual Growth
Witness	Organizer Office Administrator Teacher and Visitor
Service	Community and Social Involvement Priest and Preacher

Support   Organizer
                                 Community and Social
                                 Involvement
                                 Office Administrator
                                 Teacher and Visitor

Exploring these intersections will be especially fruitful as you zero in on how the pastor's skills can most effectively be applied to advancing the ministry goals of the total congregation.

Another principle to keep in mind is that persons should become involved in those areas of the congregation's life which parallel their skills and interests. The story is told of a public school musician who volunteered to serve on his congregation's worship and music committee. He was a willing worker and regularly was assigned the task of counting the offering. Though he was effective, it did not relate either to his primary skills or to his motivation for volunteering to serve. After a year or so he resigned from the committee.

PLANNING AND DOING

An abundance of resources is available to assist pastor and congregation in planning for ministry. Congregational planning is a complex and essential activity. It takes the congregation's visions and dreams, rubs these against the realities of the situation and resources, lays out clear steps, times, and accountabilities, and then initiates and carries out the plan.

After the planning, of course, comes the doing. Pay particular attention to how much freedom is given to persons and groups to pursue their own assigned responsibilities. Research indicates that one of the valued aspects of the ordained ministry is that the pastor ordinarily has a great deal of work freedom—the freedom to decide how a responsibility can best be fulfilled, and then to pursue it with a minimum of interference. This finding might suggest that individual lay members and committees also appreciate and profit from sufficient room in which to pursue their responsibilities.

41

EVALUATION AND RECOGNITION

No shared ministry is responsible, reflective, or fun without evaluation and recognition. Evaluation is probably the most ignored part of the planning process. It usually happens after the action is over, and is something like washing the dishes and cleaning up after a banquet has been served. But as you know, washing the dishes and reflecting with others about what happened at the meal is often productive, even enjoyable.

Without pressing the example too far, evaluation and recognition are somewhat like that. They provide the time to say: What did we try to do and how well did we do it? How will we readjust next time? We ask the question from all sides: What have we learned from this particular experience of shared ministry that will help us in our future plans?

Don't forget the recognition. Don't forget the fun. The church is not a place of sadness and gloom but the focal point of the joyous love of God. So then, a certain lightheartedness ought to mark our work together. Our Lord has guaranteed the ultimate victory, so our little victories are reflections of Easter and deserve their celebrations. And even our most dismal failures pale and stand insignificant before Calvary—and therefore deserve only moderate remorse and breastbeating. Let us learn from them and then forget them.

I know a worship and music committee that has a party and celebration at their first meeting after the busy, sometimes hectic Christmas season. After the trees are trimmed, concerts sung, pageants performed, and Christmas visitors made welcome, it is time for a party. What a good idea and a robust recognition for some work well done! Such an event is a tangible acknowledgment that in shared ministry we are concerned both with task and with people. Accomplishing the task is insufficient by itself. Celebrating fills the cup of accomplishment to the brim.

ROADBLOCKS TO SHARED MINISTRY

There are a few key things to watch out for on the road to shared ministry. The most typical problems come in three areas:

unclear congregational goals, unclear pastoral roles, and poor climate.

Goals must be worked out with care and attention appropriate to the size and complexity of the congregation and its perceived mission. The matter of establishing clear and workable goals is never a quick or easy task, even in the smallest congregation. Discouragement can come. Lack of interest can prevent even a beginning. But without clear goals, real shared ministry happens only with luck, and the odds are not very good.

Unclear pastoral roles are the same sort of thing. They, along with congregational goals, are the two basic content elements in shared ministry. If the focus on pastoral roles is fuzzy, then the whole connection between roles and goals will be unclear. What pastoral roles are most important to pastor?—to people? In what roles is the pastor most effective? Once these questions are answered, you are ready to interface the pastoral roles with your congregational goals and to begin visioning and planning.

Poor climate is more complicated, but it too can be dealt with. If things just keep grinding to a halt and it seems impossible to move toward shared ministry, it may be that pastor, congregation, or both don't really want to have a shared ministry. Remember the description of the casual-friends and stalemate congregations? They both have climate problems. In one case lethargy is the primary problem, and in the other distrust and antagonism. There are some other climate problems, and any of them is capable of inhibiting or preventing shared ministry.

To identify what the climate problem may be, call together the pastor and a few trusted lay members. Take the risk of being honest with each other. Be willing also to be nonjudgmental and open to other ideas. It might be helpful to bring in an outsider to assist in clarifying and mediating the issues. It is worth the effort and the pain involved in such a climate testing. At stake is reclaiming and renewing a ministry and moving together to new goals and new levels of sharing. A poor climate almost never goes away by itself. Both pastor and people experience the confusion, diversion of energy, frustration, discouragement, and pain it causes. Not addressed, climate problems usually precipitate open conflict with even more serious consequences for all.

STAYING ON TRACK

Even good shared ministries, like good marriages, pass over rough places and need renewal. Keeping any relationship going requires conscious effort from time to time. Without renewal, a shared ministry degenerates.

How do you stay on track? You do it by planning opportunities and techniques for reviewing and renewing the shared ministry. At least once a year a fresh appraisal should be made of the goals and roles established in the previous year. A good time to do this is two or three months after new congregational leaders are elected. Get new information from pastor and people. Review and update what has been accomplished in the past year.

Another excellent way of monitoring progress and staying on track is the pastor-parish relations committee. This committee of about five lay members and the pastor meets as often as necessary to provide support and communication. It stays in touch with how the pastor's part of shared ministry is going. It examines issues related to climate, workload, and any emerging trends in the congregation's life that affect the pastor. Such a committee can be extremely important to pastor and congregation alike.

Sometimes bringing in an outside consultant can be quite helpful in renewing shared ministry. This person might be a judicatory staff person, a skilled neighboring pastor or lay member, or a paid professional consultant. Whatever the stimulus, the responsibility for maintaining a shared ministry remains with those people who share it. They are the actors, theirs is the ministry, and hence the responsibility is theirs as well.

SHARED MINISTRY OR SEPARATE MINISTRIES?

We asked this question as the chapter began, and we return to it now. We have sketched the framework of a ministry which is understood, articulated, carried out, reflected upon, and renewed as a shared effort between pastor and people. Such a ministry almost seems to flow as a whole piece when certain pastors link up with certain congregations. It can be like magic when that happens.

But most of us must make the magic happen. We hope, but we also plan; and we pray while we work. Shared ministry is both work and magic. The outline of the work is here. The magic is in you and in the doing.

When lay leaders considered the various tasks of the pastor, they, like the pastors, clustered them into six roles. There was a remarkable consistency between the lay leaders' list and the pastors' list. But we continue to hear of conflicts between pastors and their congregations. We used to assume that these problems were caused by vastly different views of what constituted the ministry. Growth in Ministry findings seemed to contradict that assumption. We went to Jim Dittes and asked, "If there is essential agreement between pastors and laity on what roles the pastor should assume, why are conflicts still popping up?" His chapter suggests that the real conflicts sprout from the seemingly small, usually unmentioned assumptions that clergy and laity make about each other. This chapter offers a challenge to plumb the depths of these perceptions and expectations.—*Editor*

4

Why Conflicts?

JAMES DITTES

"Call regularly (though perfunctorily) in our homes, but don't stay too long," say the people.

"That's spiritual gigolo work. I have important ministry to do," answers the minister.

"Ministers aren't what they used to be," retort the people; "they don't care about ministering."

"Get my wife to stay home more and attend better to the family and out of her outside things," says a church member. Or: "Get my kids off of drugs and back into school."

"That's spiritual errand-boy work," answers the minister, "or troubleshooter, and I am neither errand boy nor troubleshooter. I am your minister. I am ready to help you think through what these changes in life-style mean to you and to them and, if you dare, what they mean to God."

"I know what the problem is, and the solution, and your job is to use your words and authority, and the Bible if you can, to make that solution happen," says the church member.

"It's not the minister's job to implement your solution, or even to accept your definition of the problem, and it's not the minister's job to become your problem solver. It is the minister's job to help you explore more deeply what and where the problems are until they begin to unfold more thorough solutions; to help you wrestle until the wrestling yields its blessing. It is the minister's job to help you become a better problem finder and a better problem solver than you are." So says the minister.

"Try to think some about the sermon topic," pleads the minister, with little hope but no little bitterness; "maybe even read the Bible text in advance, and maybe even stay around afterward and have a discussion about it. Maybe even spend Tuesday evenings in a Bible study and discussion group. This *is* a church, you know."

"That was a cute illustration about babies," defy the people, "but I do think your sermons should be shorter. And you understand, of course, that I need to keep Tuesday evening to watch M*A*S*H—family time, you know."

"Have you seen the flashy car the minister drives?" whisper the people, "and the low-cut dress his wife wore to the party the other night? But at least she does take phone messages for him, and he still spends all day Monday visiting nursing homes."

"Don't make me your paid holy one and good-deed doer, your sexless suffering servant," grumbles the minister, probably to himself. "That might ease your conscience, but I am liberated from that small-town, small-mind, super-meek stereotype. I am your minister, intended and intending to be potently intrusive into your life and conscience, not the mild scapegoat to be sent off into the desert to balm your conscience."

"That's an interesting idea, a lady minister, and you do look good in those pulpit robes. But I just don't think a lady minister would fit into this church," the pulpit committee chairman patiently explains.

"That's exactly why you need a minister like me, who can help you explore, no more gently than need be, just what your notions of 'fitness and fittingness' are, and where they come from, and why they are so narrow, and how they can be enlarged—and you, too," she answers, but probably not out loud.

"Keep off of politics and out of city hall; don't mention blacks more than every two months; don't interfere with the funeral directors' business, or any other business for that matter; read the Bible for all of us—you do it so well, and the praying, too. And for God's sake, don't start talking about civil rights for homosexuals! I want a church with a real minister!" The people issue their call over their shoulder on the way out the church door.

"How can I be a minister if the people will not be a church," says the minister, on the way out the other door.

In the partnership between minister and people in trying to fashion Christian community, there is seldom anything important about how they go about that partnership which is not in dispute. But hardly the open dispute I have expressed here. The words may sound familiar to church people—lay and clergy— but they will not often have heard them, much less uttered them. They actually will have accosted each other in much more muted and disguised fashion. The dispute between people and minister about how they are each to enact their part of the partnership must be one of the last secret shames our society harbors. Alcoholism and other addictions, mental illness, joblessness, unwed motherhood, even theological doubts—all such fallings-away from the conventional standards of good citizenship and good churchmanship are out of the closet and openly accepted as postures some people find themselves in, postures which are not excluded from the church. These things have become part of the prayerful "concerns of the church," just as the Christian church has long since embraced in its concern other postures—the ill and the dying and the aging—that are regarded as so disruptive in some cultures. But not so that seeming threat to the fabric of the church in the bitter and basic disagreements between people and minister as to how they are to relate to each other. The prayer book offers nothing under the rubric "Role Conflict" between clergy and laity, either as confessional or intercessory prayer.

This chapter will make bold to suggest that such prayers be offered under the rubric of "Thanksgiving," thanksgiving for the creative energies in refashioning and maturing of church and ministry which can be unlocked when these "role conflicts" are unlocked and brought out of the closet.

But that is difficult. The myth of the harmonious Christian community is fiercely entrenched still: the loving, faithful people of God committed to the loftiest of ideals and to each other. We need this myth—apparently we need it far more desperately than the other myths which have in the past yielded to our courage and to our need to grapple with problems in the open.

We are now learning to accept, welcome, and harness the long-suppressed power of conflict and tension in other areas of our lives. Conflicts within an individual; between differing wants and needs; conflicts between a man and a woman in intimate union; conflicts between parents and children; between different ethnic groups, political factions, and economic interests—all these conflicts we acknowledge and accept as normal. We even welcome them as the creative tension necessary in the long run for life and growth, even though in the short run they may be painful and disruptive.

But these conflicts are not yet welcomed or (if possible) permitted in the church. We must still desperately need the church as our symbol of harmony and rest in the midst of the storm.

In fact, disagreements, or "role conflicts," within the community of the faithful, have been a standard and expected part of church experience from its beginning and in all places. Such conflict has provided a welcome occasion for creative growth. Where there is conflict, there is commitment—people care. Where there is conflict, there is energy, energy available to be deployed. Where there is conflict, there are messages and calls to be heard. What people have to say to each other in this disagreement, although often difficult to hear and often coded or disguised or muted, contains corrections or insights or questions or answers which are needed. Where there is conflict, there is possibility of newness and enhancement. Old ways which are good but incomplete can be left behind in favor of new ways which are forged in the openness of the conflict.

From the first conversation between church committee and candidate, the people of the church and their minister assume a harmony, look for congruence and agreement, overlook and suppress conflict. When disagreement becomes too obvious to suppress, they suppose it to be a flaw, a delinquency, something abnormal and unusual, somebody's fault, a scandal.

At the outset of his ministry, a ministry which was to climax with the saving painful action of the cross, Jesus was subjected to many temptations in the wilderness. The final offer of the devil, according to Luke, was to act as though he were free of conflict or other pain, to act as though "the angels will take care of you; not even your feet will be hurt on the stones." So too at the end of his ministry, Jesus was subjected in Gethsemane to the same temptations to let the painful cup pass.

Any minister knows and frequently succumbs to the temptation to assume or court an immunity, a kind of 4-D exemption from all warfare large and small—a kind of absolute pacifism in all events. Yet such ministers are serving in the name of One who rejected the temptations for immunity and protection; One whose ministry moved by surprise and conflict by using the deliberate ambiguity of parables and by the deliberate confrontation with the established ways of religion; One who was consistently misunderstood and deserted and betrayed by his disciples as by his opponents; One who knew that he *had* to be misunderstood and deserted in order to reach the people; One who knowingly turned his face toward anguish; One who points us to the life which is beyond the end of life.

The Growth in Ministry Project participated in the general conspiracy to cover up conflict by not including any research questions about it. Neither clergy nor spouse nor lay people were asked to say anything about disputes or disagreements of any kind, much less disputes about the way ministers shape their work. We have no direct information about what role conflicts these Lutherans perceive or how they think about them. Yet the project does recognize the reality of conflict by including this chapter in its book. The data permit us to infer where some potential conflicts lie in the ways that the clergy and the lay people perceive the roles of ministers.

The disagreements are not about *what* the minister does and should do. As chapter 2 suggested, there is essential agreement in the basic structure of the roles. Members of these churches and their clergy would all give much the same list of the activities of ministry: priest and preacher, community and social leader, organizational enabler, and so forth. There may be disagreement—we all know that there is—in the priority that different people would assign to these roles. Some clergy may very well want to give more emphasis to community and social leadership and less emphasis to organizational work than some of their members want them to. But there are no data to demonstrate this difference in priorities. In any case, such conflicts are relatively overt, talked about, and reasonably well dealt with. The conflicts which this project does help us to recognize more clearly are conflicts which are much more subtle and less well recognized. They are the more nuanced disagreements about *how* clergy conduct these roles. In particular, the rest of this chapter will focus on the two conflicts that seem most suggested by the data.

One of these conflicts has to do with the minister's role in counseling—how differently the minister and the lay people define their expectations as to what that counseling is all about and how it should proceed. In brief, it may be that the lay people mostly want the minister simply to be present, to spend time with them, as a symbol of holiness and as a bringer of blessings. By contrast, the minister is seeking more depth and substance in his or her definition of counseling and personal visiting. The minister perceives the visiting and counseling as requiring a skill to be close to people, whereas the people are more likely to perceive the minister as a representative of those holy things from which they feel distanced. This is all suggested in the research data by the fact that the lay people tend to lump together all counseling and visiting, emphasizing more the verb than the object of the verb; the ministers make sharp distinctions as to different kinds of counseling. I think the point is better illustrated in the kind of hypothetical case which shall be presented shortly.

Why Conflicts?

The other conflict suggested by the data has to do with the expectations about how a minister proceeds to assist organizations and groups in the church. Again, the issue is partly a matter of relative superficiality versus relative depth. The lay people are more inclined to expect the minister to assist overtly with staffing their projects, doing the paperwork and the managing and the convening, maybe even sometimes doing the work of the committee for it and saving them the trouble of meeting. Ministers are more inclined to see their role as a deeper, behind-the-scenes enabling, not so much doing the lay people's work for them as providing the kind of support and guidance that makes them more able to do it. This conflict is suggested in the data by the fact that lay people include two extremely overt "management" items along with the other "enabling" items, while the clergy separate the two management items ("manages the church office," "helps manage church finances") in a quite separate factor from the "enabling" items ("works with congregational board and committees," "recruits, trains, and assists lay leaders and teachers"). That lay people see these management activities as comparable with "working with" defines more what they mean by "working with." But again, I think the point is better made in the hypothetical case which follows.

The types of conflicts between clergy and laity which are most dramatic—disagreement over political or economic issues, or (at least once upon a time) over theological issues—these conflicts get more notice, probably because they are really more tolerable. They also give the parties more chance to practice heroics; each side can take a strong public stand on mighty principles. But the kinds of conflicts we are dealing with here are more irksome because they seem more trivial and unnecessary. It seems that with just a little clarification, goodwill will straighten things out. But they are also more irksome because they are actually more frustrating and sabotaging of ministry than the more dramatic kinds. These conflicts also remain more covert—real sabotage has to be. The more trivial and seemingly accidental and incidental conflicts can be left unrecognized.

These incidental, trivial, irksome, covert conflicts issue intimately out of the significant and urgent concerns of everyday life. That is why they must be kept disguised; they are so loaded. That is why they are so important to attend to; they are fraught with meaning and possibilities for significant address and ministry.

A BIBLE STUDY FOR FIRST CHURCH

When George Russell and the search committee of First Church had the day-long interview, before the church called him to be their minister, the committee and George were nearly ecstatic at the rapport they discovered and at the hopes for a fruitful collaboration as minister and as church. "Here are people who really want to take the church seriously," George told his wife jubilantly, still smarting and burning over the frustrations in his present ministry, which so often seemed to consist of prodding people into doing what they should be doing. "For example, they liked the idea of a study group that will get serious about the Bible and about contemporary issues."

"Here is a minister that really wants to take some leadership and do new things," said the search committee, congratulating themselves on their find, still smarting and burning from their recent experience with a minister who seemed to go into retreat and to abdicate effective leadership. "Especially, did you notice his enthusiasm and initiative in the way he wants to get a study group going?"

There is no role conflict here. The pastor and the lay leaders agree, even with relief and enthusiasm, on what they want their minister to be doing. They agree, for example, on this study group as an important project, and they agree that the minister should "supply ideas for new activities and projects," "recruit, train, and assist lay leaders," "work with congregational boards and committees," "map out objectives," and "promote and create enthusiasm for church activities." They agree that these are an important role for the minister, a role which the Growth in Ministry Project has labeled *enabler,* a label George Russell will probably also use but not the search committee, who are more likely to say "leader" or "organizer" or perhaps "manager." If there are any hints of conflict or disappointment to come, minister and committee overlook them and emphasize, jubilantly, their rapport and hope.

But even in this very enthusiasm which George Russell and the search committee first felt there are the seeds for disappointment, including the disappointment in each other that will look like role conflict.

A year later George Russell and members of the church have very different stories to tell their spouses when they get home from an evening meeting of the study group. Each feels let down by the other. "They don't really want a study group—that would take work," George tells his wife. "They don't really want to dig into the issues. They want me to do it all for them. They want to spend more time talking about when we should have the next meeting and whether we should serve coffee before or after."

"George just seems to leave us drifting," one of the group members says to another on their way out.

"Yes, he just doesn't seem to be prepared," the other replies. "I really don't carry away many answers from church from what he has to say."

And another, "He should have the schedule for our next meeting all arranged, and also have somebody already assigned to make coffee so we don't have to spend so much time talking about that."

Is this role conflict? Yes, because the disappointment comes from differing expectations about *how* a minister will go about "leading" this study group. George is basically more concerned with the process than with any product. He is concerned that individual members, and the group itself, mature in their ability to define and grapple with important issues of faith and of Christian responsibility. His ideal is that the group should grow to be able to get along without him. So he deliberately, as one way of "working with" them (a way, in fact, much recommended in his seminary and in books on pastoral theology), stands back and leaves room for them. He answers questions with more questions intended to sharpen and motivate the questioner's own perceptions. But the group members expect him to answer questions with clear answers they can carry home. George deliberately leaves planning for the group life to them in such things as scheduling and coffee making, but they expect him to be the manager and to "staff" the group. In George's view, it is *their* group and *their* church, and he is their *minister*—meaning, to him, one who can assist them in focusing and channeling their energies and commitments, but not one who has to create their energies and commitments or to substitute his own for them. In their view, it is *George's* group and in important ways *George's* church, and they are there to be his *assistants* or *supporters,* rather than the other way around.

George expects to affect their lives more deeply and more permanently than they expect. They want him to be more immediate and visible and practical in his effect on their lives. He feels them to be superficial and to be resisting his ministry. They feel him to be remote and resistant to their needs and requests. They want the study group and his work with it to be as concrete and "helpful" as keeping records and correspondence and as managing church finances. This is exactly what George does not want his ministry with the group to be. The purpose of this study group, and the purpose of his work with all church groups, is to penetrate below the mundane level of finances and record keeping on which so much of their lives is lived and to define the deeper issues and resources which can transform these mundane lives—in church activities and out.

It is a role conflict if we think of it as a disagreement about how a minister will conduct himself. Perhaps more accurately, it is a profound and important difference about the nature of church and ministry and the life to which God calls people. What seems like irksome and trivial discontent over irksome and trivial details of the group life is in fact rooted in profound expectations about the nature of church and ministry, and of God's intentions and resources. The postmeeting griping which "should not belong in a church" actually encodes important theological expectations and convictions which precisely *do* belong in church discussion.

It becomes a question as to whether or not minister and people can recognize and address these issues which are latent in what they are saying to and about each other. There are at least five things a minister can do about such conflict. He or she can (1) *deny and defy* it or can (2) *capitulate* to it. He or she can (3) try to *win* it or (4) be willing to *lose* it. Or (5) the minister can *learn* from it and *minister* with and through it. All are, unhappily, common reactions, except perhaps the fifth.

DENY AND DEFY. George can complain to his wife or to his fellow clergy and, after this catharsis, get it off his chest and forget his complaints. In this way he in effect supposes that they or he "just had a bad night" or that the problem was somehow transient or accidental and not really important to acknowledge. He will swallow his own disaffection, feeling somehow guilty for being critical. He will preserve the myth of harmony in the church. He will persevere all the more in his own plans and style, assuming that they will prevail, and cling to those small shreds of success ("Elmer did come up with a remarkable biblical insight the other week") which he will soothe himself with, brag to his colleagues about, and maybe use as a kind of club over Elmer and other members to keep them up to this par.

By contrast to denying and defying the conflict, the way in which to *minister* with it insists on being honest about the conflict and about the feelings it arouses. Even more important, it insists that the conflict is real and not an accident, that people are conducting themselves as they are for reasons that are important to them and important to know about.

CAPITULATE. Rather than suppressing the conflict, the minister can give it sovereignty. George can give up his attempts at ministry because they prove just as frustrating and unsuccessful as he says they are. He can assume that the conflict and resistance that he feels is bigger than he and his commitments and his resources. He may overtly abandon the study group or the church or the parish ministry or his faith; although more commonly, he will continue going through the motions but protectively leave his energies and commitment and heart out of it.

By contrast, the way of ministering with conflicts recognizes these as quite finite. They are measurable. They have a beginning which can be discerned and which has a meaning and message in it, and they have an end which can be reached by dealing with the sources and causes. The conflict may be a symptom, yes, but is only a symptom and therefore a clue to diagnosis and treatment, not occasion for abandoning and sacrificing the patient.

Win. George can take his grievances, and the perceptions which they reflect, at face value. He can scold the group members for their delinquencies, can remind them of the commitments they made and his perception of what those commitments meant, and he can try to recall them to conduct themselves in the way he thinks they should, and thought they had agreed to, the way which will support his understanding of his ministry. "Take more responsibility, work harder, read these books, be brighter . . ." Be suitable and responsive, "enablees" fitting my style of enabling ministry.

Lose. This is probably the most common response to such conflict. The minister succumbs to the implied expectations and does things "their way." He will arrange for meetings and for coffee, and will deliver lectures and answer their questions with something they can carry away.

In contrast to either winning or losing, the way of ministering with a conflict does not yield to choosing up sides. Instead, it insists that minister and lay people are sharing the dilemma together.

Ministry is larger than any role conflict and is not damaged or threatened by it. Ministry recognizes the conflict as part of itself and not alien, an inevitable and useful—perhaps even God-given and God-intended—part of itself. The minister is open to learning from the conflict and to using it, looking for the ways in which the conflict re-calls to new, previously unrecognized ministry. The minister does not feel the conflict as an adversary, but as raw material for shaping fresh ministry. Above all, the minister does not feel the lay people who share the conflict as adversaries.[1]

"Things are not flowing the way we expected them to when we got started with such high hopes," George reflects toward the end of one session of the group. He reminds them of their initial expectations and commitments, not as a club to shape their behavior "back into line" but simply as a benchmark from which they can all measure their present shared plight. There is not scolding in his voice but invitation. His finger is not pointing at them but is scratching his head.

Yet they nevertheless deal with the plight with some denial and some defensiveness: "Well, no group ever goes as well as you hope it will."

"That's true. And I am not particularly upset. But I wonder whether there may not be some special things that we should notice that are happening to us in this particular group which we can understand and learn from." George can accept the conflict as real but not as sovereign, and he wants to help the group stay open to it. "How would you describe the difficulties we seem to be having here?"

After denials from some members who are not used to acknowledging conflict or any other distress, if they can help it— "I don't see anything wrong . . . the group is doing just fine . . . we just need to keep at it . . ."—George tries to help them all focus on the situation and its message. "How would you describe our disappointments?"

"It often seems that we get the waters stirred up and muddy, but not cleared up." Avoiding the temptation to be defensive, George stays open and gradually helps them say that sometimes they are particularly disappointed that he does not come through with answers. But his openness is a bit contagious, and after a bit, some of the group members are doing a double take: "Sometimes you leave us so much room we hang ourselves, but sometimes in all that room we have to do our own thinking, and that is not always bad."

For his part, George comes to recognize that their need for structure and for solutions is not just some kind of perversity or obstruction to his intentions, as he had felt in his initial frustration, but is in fact a legitimate need of theirs.

So, once minister and members face the conflict squarely, they can see through their disappointments to sense each other's positions. The minister can begin to sense that the people do not have the leisure or the experience or the temperament for a more relaxed and chaotic seminar which he might have been used to in theological school. He can find ways to be a leader who provides some structure and some clarification without sacrificing his "enabling" style. The members recognize that the minister is not just backing away out of laziness but out of an intention, which they can respect and whose benefit they can recognize. They can begin to credit his style as helping them in his own way. More importantly, however, there is ministry through the conflict as minister and members discover that in this very conversation in the midst of the conflict they have achieved just that intimacy and sense of collaboration they longed for and had found frustrated. So long as they were dealing with more remote political, economic, biblical, or theological issues, working together seemed more difficult and seemed to require more unbending than they could manage. When they together face the immediate dilemma confronting them, they find themselves sharing the trust and the concern and the urgency and the openness to each other and to the Spirit which they have long sought. Instead of letting the conflict separate them and prevent them from becoming a minister and a church together— as they first felt it—they shared the conflict and let it enable them more fully to become the minister and church they aspired to.

COUNSEL FOR THE COUNSELOR

Don Larson and the board of deacons—as most Lutherans who responded to the Growth in Ministry questionnaires—thought that individual ministry in visiting and counseling parishioners was very important. So when Don was summarizing his counseling ministry to the deacons after one year in the church, he expected them to share the enthusiasm he felt and to express their approval. In one year he had earned the trust of many of his parishioners and spent long hours in his study helping them think through their dilemmas and crises. But the trustees were clearly mixed and mild in their appreciation for this ministry. "That is a lot of time for a few people . . . that doesn't leave you much time for the rest of us, does it?"

"They just don't realize how significantly I have entered into and even changed some lives," he fumed to himself and to his wife. And he was right.

"He just doesn't seem to realize how important it is for him to get around and into our homes and be present to all of us where we live," fumed some of the deacons to each other. And they were right.

There was not open complaining for Don to deal with, but only his own disappointment at their failure to recognize a part of the ministry he thought they once endorsed heartily. But this disappointment was something to take seriously. He had offered them what he thought was a record of good work in their eyes as well as in his. But they left him stranded with it. He felt this way for several days after that deacons' meeting. But after he got past thinking about what the confrontation had meant to him—real disappointment and hurt (role conflict, if you will)—he became able to wonder what this confrontation meant to the deacons, what they were saying about themselves, and what they seemed to be saying about him. So, at the next deacons' meeting, he decided to ask them. He did not pout about his disappointment and what they had done to cause it, but he put it out on the table for all to see and to wonder about. "Last time, I noticed you were not very enthusiastic about my report about counseling. I think maybe you were trying to tell me something."

There were the usual scrimmages and sprinkling of denials that are common when people are not accustomed to facing conflict that openly. But the same minister who had earned the trust of many counselees also essentially had the trust of these deacons, and they could respond to his openness with an openness of their own.

"It means a lot to have the pastor come around to our house, at least once a year, even if it is only for a few minutes. After all, you are the pastor, and it brings a blessing into our house to have you there. . . . If you are spending all of your time in the office with people getting divorced, then you don't have any time to come and keep our families together. . . ."

"But I can't get to know you in a few minutes in your house in an important way," Don protested. "That is like asking me to give a blessing at the men's dinner but not giving me a chance to say anything or meet any of you." Don meant the comparison to indicate how trivial and irrelevant this "holy man" assignment left him. But the deacons picked it up as illustrating their point: "That is exactly right. Having that blessing is important."

Gradually the deacons came to speak more explicitly of their need for living symbols of the divine presence from which they so easily felt estranged. Don could recognize this as a legitimate need and not simply as childish religion or a trivializing of his role or an avoidance of the more earnest and substantial counseling relationship he sought for. To play the role of their "holy man" did not seem so different after all from responding to the important human need and yearning which he experienced in the intense counseling sessions. Don could begin to feel that their yearning for significant presence was not so different from his own yearning which he found satisfied in the intense and intimate counseling relationships. Both the deacons and Don yearned to touch deeper dimensions of life and of God's creative presence in that life. That congruence turned out to be far more important than the initial "conflict" over finding his presence in different ways. It also turned out to be far more constituting of church and ministry together than the initial differences seemed to threaten their aspirations to be minister and the church.

Most importantly, however, this very exchange—facing honestly and together a small crisis in their common life—gave them an enlivening sense of presence and power. It introduced a sense of being part of God's creative healing. This was exactly what the deacons had wanted in the symbol of a pastor's presence in their home, and what Pastor Larson had wanted in touching deeply the distress and its undoing in the intense counseling sessions. "Imagine thinking the Spirit was really present in a deacons' meeting!" one exploded with delight. "In a deacons' meeting in which we started bickering with the pastor," another pointed out. Exactly so.

To dedicate one's life to something which returns no satisfaction is to invite trouble. Harold Lohr begins his chapter by inviting us to agree that it is alright to seek satisfaction in the ministry. Yet there are those who will reply, "You are not in the ministry to be satisfied, but to serve." But for those who follow Dr. Lohr's reasoning, there may emerge a definition of satisfaction which isn't self-centered but rather provides continued impetus to serve others. The Growth in Ministry findings indicated that most pastors are fairly satisfied. That itself may be something of a surprise to anyone who has heard the complaining of a group of pastors as they express their exasperation with the way things are going. Most remarkable, though, is how pastors tend to find satisfaction. These factors are described on the following pages and are likely to provide a good bit of food for thought.—*Editor*

5

Satisfaction?!

HAROLD LOHR

If you and I can agree on the way I am going to use a word, we'll have a better chance of understanding each other. Before discussing that word, I'll take the chance of writing it. The word is *satisfaction*.

Did I lose you already? I may have if you are skeptical when people use secular language to talk about pastoral ministry. It's not that the word isn't a fine word. It's the context.

You may object because satisfaction suggests an ego trip for the clergy, a ministry that feathers the pastor's own nest. A "What's in it for me?" attitude has no place in persons who are the disciples of Jesus Christ.

I agree. Jesus says that his ministry—and that of his followers —is not for personal reward. He had to correct that misunderstanding among his own disciples.

Remember, for example, Jesus' brief exchange with the sons of Zebedee and their mother (Matt. 20:20–28). Those young men, at their mother's prompting, indulged in some satisfying fantasy as they daydreamed about the pleasure of sitting at the Lord's right and left hands in the kingdom.

"It shall not be so among you," said Jesus; "but whoever would be great among you must be your servant, and whoever would be first among you must be your slave; even as the Son of man came not to be served but to serve, and to give his life as a ransom for many."

That takes care of self-aggrandizement. When we talk about satisfaction among the clergy, we don't mean that.

Satisfaction is also suspect when it implies an end in itself. The Bible traces God's ongoing intervention in human history.

He finally becomes human himself to get the message across firsthand. "I love you. I can give you joy and show you the purpose of life." Christians are people who have got that message, who know that the meaning of life is in God's purpose for it.

But human beings don't always hear very well. And human will is obstinate. In increasingly sophisticated ways, people are tempted to put stone upon stone, building their private altars, and then to scramble up on them to await the praise that belongs to God. Human efforts and accomplishments can become diversions, turning attention from God to self. There is nothing new in that. That is the self-satisfaction of the stereotypical Pharisee.

When we discuss satisfaction in ministry we are not promoting self-idolatry. Neither will self-aggrandizement and self-righteous pride be baptized here.

WHAT IS SATISFACTION?

But there is a different kind of satisfaction.

Meet Frank Bates, for example. Frank is a senior at Alpona High School, and he can run faster than anyone in town. When he was a freshman, people already knew he was a winner. That was the year he smashed the county record for the hundred-yard dash. Just under ten seconds! And that time still stands for freshmen in Pierce County.

Frank is self-disciplined. For five years he has been getting up with the sun—when the sun has made it. And even when the sun has slept late, hidden by rain or snow, Frank has strained one foot in front of the other for five miles before breakfast, sloshing or slipping, but always determined. He counts calories, but he burns them off twice as fast as you or I. And at ten at night, Frank's in bed.

When no one else is on the track, Frank is there, sometimes alone, sometimes with his coach: practicing his starts, getting the rhythm just right, releasing that last agonizing burst of speed, shaving a few more hundredths of a second off his best time, competing against the clock and against himself.

Why does he do it?

"The one gift I have," says Frank, "is the ability to run. And I'm going to make the most of it.

"Maybe I'll get an Olympic tryout. There have been a few scouts around, you know.

"Nothing is more satisfying to me than to blast off when I hear the starting gun. I'd be a bum if I didn't fine-tool my gift. Win or lose, man!—I put all of me into the race. That's what it's all about!"

And then there's Debbie Allen.

Debbie is a nurse. She bathes sick people, gives shots, watches heart blips on an electronic monitor, and gets sore feet from walking the corridors in the intensive care unit of Mercy Hospital.

Always wanting to be a nurse, Debbie earned an associate degree at Radford Community College. She excelled in her state boards, received her R.N., went to work at Mercy, and then enrolled in a night-school bachelor's degree program at nearby State University.

"I can't think of any profession that would be more satisfying for me," says Debbie. "But I still have so much to learn before I can help people who need my best. I get tired of the bedpans and sometimes I get so depressed by all the pain and suffering around me. But what is more satisfying than to do what you're good at and to know that your work is important—that *you* are important—to people who need you?"

Both Frank and Debbie know about satisfaction. They experience it. It's what comes with doing what is important to you and doing it the best you can. And it is doing the important in spite of the debits on the other side of the ledger: straining your muscles, getting up at dawn, sacrificing other pleasant things because you have your goal, going to school with the demands of a family and a job, gagging on the smells of medicine and human bodies, keeping calm after still another complaint.

But satisfaction, as we now use the word, promises no easy life. Indeed, part of the satisfaction comes from realizing that the cost of doing something important (to you) is a necessary part of reaching worthwhile goals. That keeps you disciplined.

We even dare to use the word, defined this way, to speak of Jesus. Just before his death, knowing what was to come, Jesus prayed, "But now I am coming to thee; and these things I speak in the world, that they may have my joy fulfilled in themselves.

I have given them thy word; and the world has hated them because they are not of the world, even as I am not of the world" (John 17:13–14).

So the writer of the Letter to the Hebrews speaks of discipleship, saying, "Let us run with perseverance the race that is set before us, looking to Jesus the pioneer and perfecter of our faith, who for the joy that was set before him endured the cross, despising the shame" (Heb. 12:1–2).

Let us call one last witness. Second Timothy 4:7 reports the Apostle Paul, about to die, reflecting upon his ministry: "I have fought the good fight, I have finished the race, I have kept the faith." This man who, more than any other, has kept the church straight on the meaning of grace, the gift of God in Jesus Christ, does not now discount his own commitment to his ministry and his full use of his talents in Christ's cause. At the end of his life his great satisfaction centers in his faithful response, over many years, to God's call. He has given everything that was in him, and it is a satisfying way to complete his life.

We do not apologize, then, for affirming that satisfaction is valid in those who enlist themselves in the ministry of Jesus Christ. There is something incongruous about pastors who are not excited about the message entrusted to them. The good news announces that life is beautiful and purposeful. Ambassadors for Christ represent the risen Lord! To be called to this office and then to fill it is to participate in a truly satisfying and fulfilling life.

SATISFACTION VERSUS DISSATISFACTION

Our central theme, then, is satisfaction. Let us become more specific as we relate satisfaction to pastoral ministry.

Maybe it would be helpful to review a recent week in terms of satisfaction and dissatisfaction. On a separate sheet of paper, draw vertical lines so that you have three columns. Label them as shown in the diagram. Construct a horizontal numbered scale, as indicated, for each activity you enter.

Now reflect on your week for ten to fifteen minutes. As you think of the major activities you have carried out, jot them down in the first column.

ACTIVITIES	DISSATISFYING	SATISFYING	WHY

```
            3   2   1   0   1   2   3
            +---+---+---+---+---+---+
            3   2   1   0   1   2   3
            +---+---+---+---+---+---+
```

You might list, for example, "prepared and preached Sunday sermon"; "counseled with George Billings about his job"; "filled out quarterly report for mission board"; "conducted funeral service for Bill Jarvis"; "argued with spouse about family budget."

When you have completed your list, go back and think about each activity. Was it satisfying or dissatisfying? To what degree? Mark the scale in the second column at the point that gives a measure of your satisfaction or dissatisfaction. In the last column, write a brief reason for each rating.

The pastor who provided the examples above might have rated "counseled with George Billings about his job" as satisfying, giving it a 3 on the right side of the scale, because "I was able to help George sort out some important life decisions."

This same pastor might have put a 3 on the other end of the scale for "argued with spouse about family budget," because "we never agree about how to spend our inadequate salary." (Finish this exercise before reading farther.)

More than a decade ago, the industrial psychologist Frederick Herzberg studied the motivation of employees. He found that satisfaction and dissatisfaction are not really opposite ends of a common scale at all.

He discovered that people tend to identify dissatisfying elements in a job as those which, if unmet, will make people dissatisfied. If they are met, however, these factors will not make people satisfied; they only keep people from being dissatisfied.

The dissatisfiers tend to define the *work environment*: organizational policies; work conditions; salary; status; security; and relationships with supervisors, peers, and subordinates.

So workers who grumble about salaries which are too low

69

are dissatisfied. But increase the salary and you don't make the job satisfying. You only succeed in reducing the level of grumbling.

Therefore, Herzberg called the dissatisfiers "hygiene factors," because, like public health measures (sewage disposal, water purification), they don't make people healthy; they only keep people from getting sick.

Satisfiers, however, Herzberg found, tend to describe the *work itself*. They include the intrinsic interest of the work; the opportunity for achievement; recognition for the work; responsibility required in the work; and personal and professional growth gained through the work. Without these elements, people will have no satisfaction in their work.

If you did the exercise above, you may wish to review your responses. In those activities that provide satisfaction—or dissatisfaction—do you find any pattern? Do Herzberg's research findings help you to see what makes your ministry satisfying? Can you increase the time and effort you spend on satisfying activities—by sharing less satisfying ones with congregational members, for example? Do particular pastoral roles (see chapter 2) reward you more than others?

The clergy of the Lutheran Church in America and of the Lutheran Church—Missouri Synod agree substantially with Herzberg. When asked why the ministry is satisfying, they said:

"The ministry is worthwhile."

"The ministry is fascinating and challenging."

"I have freedom in my work and I like that."

"I am investing my life in work that has ultimate meaning."

These pastors differed when they were asked about their available time for ministry and the adequacy of their salary. Some felt the pressure of time; some did not. Some said their salaries were sufficient; others felt underpaid.

But these pastors did not link such factors to the ministry itself. When pastors complain about time and money, they express appropriate concern about working conditions and financial support. But they do not confuse such matters with their primary source of satisfaction, the ministry to which they have been called.

Satisfaction?!

Frederick Herzberg's research sample did not include clergy. He surveyed agricultural supervisors, teachers, technicians, nurses, food handlers, military officers, scientists, housekeepers, accountants, Finnish foremen, and Hungarian engineers; but not pastors.

Herzberg discovered that relationships with other people at work, including supervisors, were dissatisfiers. For Lutheran clergy, however, relationships are important contributors to satisfaction in ministry.

Before discussing how personal relationships, including supervision, relate to satisfaction, let me suggest another exercise.

Secure a large piece of paper—a sheet of newsprint or a shopping bag opened up to expose its inside surface. With a felt-tip marker, draw a circle in the center of the paper. Put your name in the circle.

Now draw spokes from this circle and place other circles at their ends. In these new circles, write names of persons or groups who are important in your life and work. Who helps you to be effective in your work? And don't list only your friends. Who always gives you a bad time but keeps you on your toes? (Complete your drawing before reading on.)

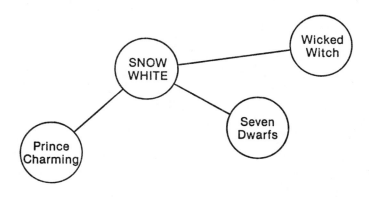

When you have written the names of your significant others, consider each in turn and below each name write the *specific* reasons that you have included them in your drawing. What do they *do* that is important? Don't give easy answers like "love"

or "support." Again, what do these people *do* specifically? What do they bring to your relationship that adds up to "love" or "support"?

Now review all the specific reasons you have written under the names. Select the five different items that are most important to you. (Count each item only once, even if it appears several times for different people.) Think about these items, asking such questions as:

Which items relate to my life, my work, or both?

Are there any significant people I forgot (my spouse, for example)? What does that mean?

Which persons (or groups) contribute most to my effectiveness?

What is the ratio of family members to congregational members? How many persons are outside my family and congregation?

How many of the items that I look for in others do I contribute to relationships myself?

Having identified what is important to support me, how can I help these relationships to grow and to build new ones?

Don't be surprised if several significant persons are members of your own congregation. It's that way for most Lutheran clergy.

SUPPORT

Pastors whose satisfaction in their ministry is like that described above also tend to value support. In recent years, experts and amateurs alike have been advocating the need for support systems for clergy. But people have disagreed about which elements are most important in support. Some say, "Pastors should build relationships with other local clergy." Others say, "Set up a pastoral relations committee in the congregation." You probably have some ideas yourself.

Jim and Nancy Olson recently attended a workshop that was designed to identify the important factors in an effective ministry. Jim has been the pastor of St. Timothy's for five years. Nancy belongs to the Lutheran Church Women and sings in the choir. She is no more involved in the church than most other active members but she knows what is going on in the congregation.

"I was surprised by my 'significant others' drawing," Jim said. "Except for our immediate family and the synod president, everyone on that paper is a member of the congregation."

"Who did you include?" Nancy asked. "And why are they important?"

"Well, honey, you made the top ten on my chart! You keep me honest. You tell me when I'm off track but you also praise things I do when I deserve it. Besides, you're a great lover!"

"You must have been copying my chart," Nancy said. "Who else?"

"I mentioned the synod president. Sam isn't around all that much, but he's there when I need him. He puts the pressure on me—with a smile—when it comes to increasing congregational benevolences. But when he meets with the church council, he pushes them on my salary and benefits. 'That's teamwork,' Sam says. And you remember when I got up on the convention floor and spoke in favor of the hunger resolution? The following week Sam called me up and told me how impressed he was with several specific points I made. And he repeated some of the things I said, so he *was* listening.

"Then I included John Glass, vice president of the church council," Jim continued. "He's my idea person. And he's a sounding board for what will fly and what won't.

"And Laura Peters. As social ministry chairperson, she is a great organizer. When a member calls up with a problem, I'm glad that Laura's around to take charge. I'd have to say that she has done more to raise my sensitivity about some community problems than four years in seminary ever did."

"Did you include Mary Franklin?" asked Nancy. "My workshop leader suggested we think about people who are significant because they are so irritating. Mary can be counted upon to be against every idea you come up with—if it's a change from 'the way we've always done it here at St. Timothy's.'"

"You got it!" Jim answered. "She got a big circle. But you know, Nancy, this exercise made me realize that Mary makes her contribution, too—although I could do without it most of the time. As I thought about some specific run-ins she and I have had, I realized that I have been doing my homework more carefully before introducing new ideas—just because I had to have a good case when she started piling on me."

"Let me tell you my great insight about your drawing, Jim," Nancy said. "My group leader really hit the nail on the head when he wrapped up this workshop experience. It's feedback that's important; that's what support is all about.

"You have named the people who tell you how you're doing. They criticize you when you need correction and they affirm you when you're on target. They trust you and you trust them. And your relationships are honest.

"How's that, hon? Am I ready to lead a workshop on my own?" she asked.

"Sign me up, Nancy."

Nancy Olson knows what support is, and she knows where parish pastors can find it. Several thousand Lutheran pastors and their spouses have shared their personal experiences, and Nancy speaks for most of them.

No one needs research to know that the support of the pastor's spouse is important. And it is clear that the pastor's own integrity and personal strength are essential.

But many do not realize that outside that context, the single most important support factor for most clergy is a network, usually informal, of co-workers in the congregation. In describing how lay members support them, pastors say:

"John is helpful in getting a job done."

"Sue is a competent person who uses her know-how for the church."

"Frank is always friendly—to me personally, and to other members of committees where he serves. Even when he disagrees, he's still my friend."

"Gloria takes a personal interest in me. I'm her pastor but she sees that I too need support and understanding. I can count on her to be sensitive when things are about to blow up, because she never forgets the human element."

Most important for support are those people who commit themselves with the pastor to the same mission, who enthusiastically use their abilities to reach the same goals. The most effective support, in other words, may be a gift. Unplanned, it may emerge and grow as pastor and lay members of the congregation do ministry together.

Although this informal network of congregational co-workers appears most frequently as the most important support factor for Lutheran clergy, other elements may also be present.

Pastors have different needs. Therefore, support systems are not likely to be identical. Some pastors may rely only upon personal integrity and inner strength. Others may desire greater diversity in their support.

On the average, however, Lutheran pastors rank the following elements as next in importance after the support of co-workers:

Value placed upon the praise of the local support group (which includes congregational lay leaders, spouse, pastors in churches of the community, other church staff members, and other close friends).

Value placed upon the praise given by judicatory support persons (pastors of the same denomination and the denominational executive who knows your work best).

Support from other professionals (which includes the same persons listed immediately above).

The difference between the last two elements is probably in the degree of concern implied by the words that are used. In the last factor, "support" is vague, although the word implies that these people can be counted upon for something. "Value placed upon the praise" of these persons ranks higher. Praise is not usually abstract; it is more likely to be directed to some specific achievement. It provides immediate feedback on performance, answering the question, "How am I doing?"

We repeat the point of this discussion. Pastors who experience satisfaction in their ministry are pastors who receive support in their ministry.

Now, if you did the exercise, look back at your own "significant others" chart. How many of the support persons and groups we have identified appear on your chart? Did you name co-workers, family members, friends outside the congregation, judicatory staff, clergy of your own denomination, clergy of other denominations?

What do these people contribute to you? Are they helpful, competent, friendly, interested in you? Do they provide feedback on your performance?

Are you satisfied with the elements in your support network? Remembering that support is focused on mutual sharing of ministry, in what ways can you increase shared ministry in your congregation and thereby build support?

SUPERVISION

Let us now discuss a related theme.

We recall that Frederick Herzberg discovered that among the employees he surveyed, supervision was a dissatisfier. That is *not* true for Lutheran clergy.

All of us know about congregations with one pastor, the only full-time employee. We also know about a smaller number of congregations with staff ministries, perhaps two or three clergy and even professional lay staff members. In the latter congregations, supervision is expected.

Let me ask you to make a guess.

What percentage of Lutheran clergy do you think would say that they are supervised in their ministry? Twenty per cent? Eighty per cent? When people have been asked that question—parish pastors, laity, bishops—their estimates have ranged from very few to many.

Two-thirds of the Lutheran clergy say they are supervised. The supervisor varies, however: the bishop, the senior pastor, the church council, the president of the church council, and unidentified others. Some pastors list their supervisor as God.

If you have completed the two exercises suggested in this chapter, you may have some personal data about supervision. Before referring to the work you have done, however, jot down the names of the people or groups you consider to be your supervisors. Then consult your "significant others" chart to identify the supervisors who appear there.

Now turn to the table you prepared to review a week of your

ministry. You identified a list of weekly activities; you rated them on a satisfaction scale; and you noted some reasons for your answers.

Examine each of your listed activities again. Is there any sense in which the activity is supervised? By whom? How does your supervisor evaluate your accountability? Are the supervised activities also satisfying?

We have already said that Lutheran pastors who experience satisfaction in their ministry tend to be pastors who have a support system. We now say further that these pastors also tend to be those who identify an effective supervisor.

"My district president is helpful to me in getting my job done."

"The senior pastor is very concerned about the welfare of those working with her."

"Trinity's board is successful in getting people to work effectively—including me."

"Our council president is competent in doing her job."

"My supervisor is friendly."

"The church council takes time at every meeting to review our mutual performance for the past month. We agree on monthly objectives and we give each other feedback on how we're doing. It's safe to talk about failures as well as successes, because we obviously are trying to improve our ministry together."

As you have been reading, you may have noticed the similarity between support systems and supervision, as we have defined each in the words that pastors use.

Support is provided by identifiable persons or groups; so is supervision.

Support persons are helpful, competent, and friendly; they provide feedback on performance. Effective supervisors have the same characteristics.

SHARING MINISTRY

Both support and quality supervision relate the pastor to people who enlist their abilities and their commitment to the achievement of mutually important goals.

We have been using contemporary language, but we have

been playing on an old and respected theme. The pastor who experiences satisfaction in ministry is the pastor who personally rediscovers the ongoing understanding that the church is the communion of saints.

God is the chief actor in the human drama. From the beginning until now, each scene has played out the tension between the loving, searching, life-giving God and obstinate human beings. We reject love; we look for meaning everywhere else but in God; we want to do it our way.

But God has sent his Son. "I'll go down and show them what I am really like and what my intentions are." So a long procession of Christians gives witness that God has closed the gap between him and us in Jesus Christ. It is a gift. We are forgiven for our sins. God sends his Holy Spirit and begins to conform our lives to the life of Jesus Christ.

The gift is God's. The response of faith is ours. But in order that such faith may come to life in each generation of Christians, one by one, God instituted the office of the ministry. That is, he gives to his church the gospel and the sacraments. The church, in turn, for the sake of good order, calls persons to the ordained ministry to represent the gospel by life, word, and action among its Christian members.

Satisfaction in the pastoral ministry is found in the ministry itself. The ministry is challenging, fascinating, of ultimate importance. It is a high calling because it deals with the things of God and with his relationship to humans.

But as we have said, the ministry belongs to the whole church. It is shared by pastors and people. In that sharing, as all give their best, mutual support develops and enhances the shared ministry of the people of God.

The ministry is not our own possession. It is God's, entrusted to his church in order that men and women may discover the abundant life in Christ and that they may minister to the needs of the world. Those who share in that ministry are certainly accountable—to God. But more immediately, they are responsible to those who on behalf of the church are entrusted with the carrying out of the total ministry—to church councils, to bishops, and to those other persons and groups who are supervisors for the Lord.

The Growth in Ministry research did not provide clear findings that relate satisfaction in ministry to effectiveness in ministry. There are hints in that research—and the many contacts with pastors, spouses, and lay leaders since the research was done do support the hunch—that those pastors who rate themselves as effective in their pastoral roles, and whose lay leaders also rate them as effective, are pastors who affirm their high satisfaction in ministry.

And why should it not be so? Satisfaction, as we have seen, *is* accompanied by support and effective supervision. But support and supervision arise in a context of shared ministry, where the performance of pastor and congregation are evaluated and where efforts are made to improve that performance.

The pastoral ministry of the Christian church is not best served by the Lone Ranger in cassock, surplice, and stole. God's gifts are received and shared in community. The pastor is part of that community. Our themes—satisfaction, support, and supervision—open up some new possibilities for sharing ministry as pastors and people and for making more personal the communion of saints among us.

Frederick Buechner observed that as the preacher waits for the sermon hymn to end and as he feels all the funny feelings of one called upon to preach, "If it weren't for the honor of the thing, he would just as soon be somewhere else." The ministry offers to all clergy an immense opportunity to respond to the "honor of the thing" in almost all its aspects. But we can get consumed by the honor and hop up on a pedestal. But as Irene Lovett suggests, this pedestal positioning can be just as much a result of the congregation's insistence as of the pastor's preference. In the following pages she offers a sound psychological analysis of why the pedestal is so alluring to clergy and what can happen to those who climb up there. There is a fine line between accepting the honor paid to the office of ministry and the need to draw one's self-image from that honor. This is a most provocative look at a constant temptation which is often treated as one of the "unmentionables" of the parish ministry.—*Editor*

6

Pastor on a Pedestal

IRENE LOVETT

Is a pastor different from the rest of the people? Margaret Adams of First Church thinks so.

"He's our spiritual leader, selected and ordained by God. God put him here to guide us. If I need an answer, he's the first one I'll ask."

"You are making him into some kind of little god, Margaret," replies her husband Don, looking up from his paper for the first time. "Jim Johnson is human, just like us. I like him, respect him even, but he's a professional and nothing more."

Jim Johnson, pastor of First Church, has a problem, but it is one he shares with all other clergy. He's not only two different people, he's of two different natures in the eyes of his people. Some members stand him on a pedestal and hang a halo over his head, while others see him as just another member of the work force trying to make a living at what he does best.

But what does Jim Johnson feel about himself? Daily he is challenged to determine what the office of ministry is. Is he the "chosen one" that Margaret perceives and wants? Does he rely on his chosenness to define his authority as a pastor? Or is he "just one of the guys," with nothing more than his particular training to separate him from the laity? Perhaps he sees himself as both.

INVESTING THE HALO

At one time the halo effect that has traditionally surrounded clergy might have been attributed to the authority they could use. P. T. Forsyth noted:

The authority of the preacher was once supreme. He bearded kings and bent senates to his word. He determined policies, ruled fashions, and prescribed thought. And yet he has proved unable to maintain the position he was so able to take. He could not insure against the reaction which has now set in as severely as his authority once did. The reaction has long been in force, and today, however great may be his vogue as a personality, his opinion has so little authority that it is not only ignored but ridiculed. In that respect the pulpit resembles the press, whose circulation may be enormous, while elections and such like show that the influence of its opinions is almost nil.[2]

The quotation is not as contemporary as it sounds. P. T. Forsyth was dean of the faculty of theology in the University of London and wrote those words at the turn of the century. It could as easily be a conclusion about today's minister. Fragmented duties and a further loss of authority set the contemporary pastor apart from those even in Forsyth's day.

The loss of authority has diminished to some extent the halo effect surrounding pastors, but has not eradicated it. The pedestal position remains in the minds of many lay persons and some pastors.

The idea that clergy are different from the general population is demonstrated in Western religion in several ways. Celibacy is required by some churches and a more stringent kind of sexual morality by others. Other professions demand evidence of academic achievement and applied practical experience, but no other expects a special setting apart, or ordination, of those who would enter.

Protestants have departed from asking their clergy to take a vow of poverty, but there remain vestigial remnants of that expectation. Few congregations assure that their pastor's salary will be equivalent to that of other professionals of similar training and experience. The sum of these expectations is that he or she is different and will get other rewards for effort.

Theologically, the assumption that a Christian minister is to exceed the congregational members in spiritual motivations and applied virtue seems based upon the confidence that those who are in ministry have heard a divine call. The New Testament Christians had not formalized the call to ministry as have those who have followed in their train. In the case of Timothy, the New Testament speaks of "the gifts within you" (1 Tim. 4:14 and 2 Tim. 1:6), and there are numerous instances of the "laying on of hands," a practice which remains a vital part of most contemporary ordination services. In its ecclesiastical sense the term *ordination*, as we interpret it, is not used in the New Testament. Normally Scripture uses the terms *appointed* or *elected*.

Protestant denominations differ in the matter of the call. Some are convinced that the call of God is channeled through the church to the individual, others believe that it comes directly from God to the individual, who then seeks the affirmation of the church.

Paul's Letter to the Roman Christians makes clear his perception of a direct personal call. "But on some points I have written to you very boldly by way of reminder, because of the grace given me by God to be a minister of Christ Jesus to the Gentiles in the priestly service of the gospel of God . . ." (Rom. 15:15–16). Not many of those who ministered in the first century spoke of the same kind of dramatic call which Paul experienced, but most certainly must have felt that it was the will of God that they should serve as they did.

Quite a mystique has been built around the call to ministry during the intervening centuries. Theological, psychological, and sociological interpretations of it have accumulated almost to the point of caricature. For some, the call has such a psychological intensity that it cannot be comprehended by anyone who has not experienced it. For them, the call is a compelling once-and-forever dictum. The call mandates that the pastor should be more dedicated—personal sacrifices more evident and inspirations more lofty—than those who engage his or her services.

R. L. Rubenstein points to this differentness.

Religion abounds in paradoxes not the least of which is the peculiar combination of arrogance and humility which so frequently marks the religious leader. He is in his own eyes privy to secrets unavailable to the multitude. He is also depressed by his own infinite lack of worth for the high charge that rests upon him. Above all, he is lonely and set apart as no other man. As a Catholic priest he may never know the most important single role available to men, that of father of a family; as a rabbi the clergyman is frequently forced to fulfill expectations of a ritual behavior demanded by his community as binding upon him but not upon them. Seldom, if ever, is the clergyman able to relax and feel that he can be himself with his people.[3]

CLAIMING THE PEDESTAL

The pastor-on-a-pedestal concept is used by both the religious community and by the pastor. Characterizing the pastor as different, someone who is more role than person (preferably wholly other or Superman), gives the congregation a focus for their tendency to idealize. There seems to be an inherent need in humankind to have a visible authority figure. This figure is a symbol of our values and ideals and is one in whom we can invest some of our dependency needs.

The pastor in the pulpit can be seen as the good father who tells us what to do and who even satisfies us with chastisement when we know we need it. This may be one of the reasons congregations have generally had some reluctance about accepting women as pastors. Traditionally, father has been head of the house and has symbolized the final earthly authority, and we have some anxiety about deposing him publicly.

Major factor or not, this idealizing and unconscious fantasizing contributes to positioning the pastor on the pedestal. However, we are at times ambivalent about the authority figures in our lives, especially our overattachments and dependencies upon them. We can be ambivalent about the halo effect surrounding the pastor also. The more emotionally mature members of the congregation may want the pastor off the pedestal and down among them as a real person who is carrying out his or her divine mission in adequate and mature ways.

The pastor may have these same mixed feelings about the

halo effect. Though it creates loneliness and puts distance between pastor and parishioners, there is a comforting quality
about being elevated. It ascribes a sense of authority whether it
delivers the real thing or not. It may temporarily relieve one of
the necessity of earning this dimension in pastoring. As long as
the pastor keeps this pose, people may listen more readily. The
pedestal can be a defensive position making one-to-one relating
less imperative. Without the pedestal, the pastor's humanity may
clearly and painfully show through.

TIP-OFF TO PERSONALITY

A pastor's reliance on the pedestal may be a tip-off to basic
personality patterning. Those who work in evaluation or therapy
with clergy suggest that there are some traits which are stronger
in ministers than in most other professionals. Perhaps Christian
ministry is particularly constituted for making those traits into
usable assets. Of course, this does not mean that ministers could
not be successful in other careers, nor does it mean that these
are the only people who can be successful ministers. It says
chiefly that these individuals are perhaps more receptive to the
call to ministry than others in a general population.

According to the psychoanalytic view, the human personality
has three major components with which to generate and handle
feelings and to respond to the world of reality. First, the id is
constituted by the basic instinctual human drives and derives
from the deep unconscious mind, which is like the hidden part
of the iceberg. Feelings emanating from the storage basement we
call the unconscious mind cannot always be dealt with comfortably. These are the very feelings most people think they've
been successful in denying.

Above the id in the hierarchy of consciousness is the ego. This
is the conscious part of us which seeks to mediate between the
deep-unconscious, feeling part of us and the world of reality.
There is a fine line standing between the id and the ego. If that
line becomes so thick that feelings and perceptions cannot pass
back and forth, we become unaware of some of the feelings

which affect our behavior. If on the other hand that line breaks down, we become unable to control ourselves.

The superego, or conscience, is a rider which extends alongside and over a part of the ego and the id. Its content is both conscious and unconscious. It is constituted by our incorporation of value-oriented teachings, admonitions, and habits. From it come the expectations we put upon others and, even more importantly, upon ourselves. It also reflects the expectations which we perceive that other significant persons have put upon us.

Clergy almost invariably seem to have an oversized superego. That conscience may incline them to be conforming and good children. Or it may have been generated by a rebellious acting-out of feelings which are later brought under control in a cataclysmic kind of conversion. Our basic traits may originate in the genetic package, stem from environmental conditioning, or develop as a combination of the two. In any case they are influenced by our early years.

All of us bring baggage from childhood. Traits and behavior can be modified, and we can come to control our feelings more than they control us. But sometimes we remain predisposed to reactions, feelings, and behaviors which were appropriate to an earlier level of development but are no longer needed. Some men and women who struggled for a sense of independence as children and adolescents do not give up the intensity of their struggle once they are chronologically mature and essentially autonomous. They need to be in authority to feel comfortable, and anyone who threatens their control imposes a threat to them. Their relationships become impaired by overdetermined behavior, behavior once necessary for emotional survival but no longer needed. So it is with the oversized superego. For a variety of reasons it can cause the pastor to seek and cherish the pedestal position. Sometimes this can impede growth and fuller development. The pedestal can represent a defensive stance with a "holy" psychological and theological overlay.

The accumulated dos and don'ts, ideals, and highest aspirations form a heavy load for a sensitive person. The load can contribute to feelings of unworthiness, incompetence, and limited self-esteem in the inner person.

When I began my work as a career counselor for the American Baptist clergy, I didn't include a specific measure of functional intelligence in the battery of psychological instruments I used. I assumed that persons who finish four years of college and three or four years of graduate work in theology are above average in general intelligence.

However, in consultations I began to feel that clergy clients did not necessarily agree with me. In an effort to introduce more reality into the evaluation, I administered the Wechsler Adult Intelligence Scale (WAIS) to the next three hundred clients. No intelligence measure is precise, but for purposes of comparison with a general population it served a useful purpose.

During the interpretation of the WAIS, each client was asked to make an informal assessment of where he or she might rank in functional intelligence. Ninety percent of these persons supposed that they functioned in the bright normal category. This was two categories below where they usually ranked. The median IQ of the group was 133, which is within the very superior range. I did not expect a specific assessment, but the difference between self-assessment and the results of the examination suggested that these clergy clients were not realistic about their intelligence resources. They seriously underestimated themselves.

THE EVALUATION TRAP

Often pastors share their discouragement about seeing so little evidence of achievement. Ministry is an undefined kind of work and varies from community to community. Measuring performance is difficult.

When life was less complex for the pastor, most people agreed that increasing budgets and membership were good criteria for measuring achievement. This is no longer necessarily true. The church and even the culture have dictated that new standards be set. A pastor may be doing a heroic and profitable ministry in a church which is growing smaller by the year.

Yet while the old standards have been discarded, new and generally acceptable ones have not emerged. There are, then, some real reasons for confusion about evaluating one's achievement.

Too many ministers, though, complicate matters even further by ignoring these hard-to-measure aspects when they look back over their failures and successes. They are aware of growing anxieties, but instead of trying to understand and relate to the root causes, they push on all the harder to be perfect. When self-expectations are too high, many clergy become workaholics. It is hard to predict whether the pedestal will produce comfortable would-be martyrs or guilt-ridden well-doers who are discouraged and weary because even their best isn't good enough.

All of this is complicated by the role to which ministers are called. An inner spiritual experience undergirds the minister's call. Unlike the medical doctor who takes the Hippocratic oath without promising to live like Hippocrates, the minister accepts a call not only to believe the faith but to model the life of Jesus. There is a fine line, though, between being an emissary of Christ and being a vicarious Christ. To those choosing the latter, the pedestal appears dangerously attractive.

DISMOUNTING THE PEDESTAL

There are routes to take in recognizing, evaluating, and avoiding the pedestal. One of the first things to recognize is that the same congregation which envisions the pastor with a pale halo over his head can use that halo as a target if it ever slips a bit. Pastors who cherish halos and pedestals are particularly vulnerable if they dare let their humanity show. It causes trouble from both within and without.

One penalty for being idealized lies in the distance it creates between pastor and people. Meaningful and sustained relationships are difficult to establish between superbeings and mere mortals. But the most devastating effect of being idealized is that it may seem to release the pastor from an effort toward personal growth. It is easier to maintain a role, even an important one, than it is to be a growing and maturely loving person.

The role playing can superficially cover the question of professional identity. The initial process of developing a self-image during childhood and adolescence later merges into the role image. Donald Super, in his self-concept theory of career development, contends that occupational development is best described as a process of developing and implementing a self-image. It is not easy for a minister to assess the interrelationship of the self, the call, and the role. The pastor who emphasizes the role rather than relationships will be defenseless against those who attempt to manipulate the idealized role to their own advantage. When this happens, genuine ministry to persons suffers.

Daniel Zeluff, for almost a decade a counselor to clergy at Interpreter's House in North Carolina, has written a small volume entitled *There's Algae in the Baptismal Font.*[4] There he caricatures various clergy attitudes about themselves and their ministries. One chapter is "I Must Be a Prophet, Else Why Are They Stoning Me?" It describes how some pastors authenticate themselves through persecution. The pastor who feels distanced from congregational members can depersonalize his own contributions to a conflict by recalling that Jesus was persecuted and that it must be expected. Living under attack is evidence of being a prophet and a person of worth. Says Zeluff, "The syndrome occurs when hostility is unconsciously, though deliberately, structured." One dodges hostility by assuming a role but at the same time dodges possible growth through constructive conflict. The only advantage is that it delays some of the pain—at least temporarily.

WAYS TO GET OFF:
THE GOOD, THE BAD, AND THE UGLY

There are ways to get off the pedestal. Some are helpful, some are unhelpful.

Keeping that pose can become depressing and anxiety-producing. The fear of falling from the lofty estimate of others or of being discovered to be human can be threatening. Sometimes the pedestal shakes a little and there come awful moments of insight when fallibility is keenly felt. There is a conflict between what *seems to be* and what *is*.

When that happens, emotional tensions surface, and when they begin to be too excessive to endure, the pastor can leap from the pedestal to avoid the pain. The consequences are not rationally considered. The goal is to escape pain. The tension may result in a regression to adolescent behavior, sometimes into the unacceptable moral type.

But there can be other results. Seemingly positive relationships can be fractured by the unmodulated release of anger. Sometimes blame is projected upon others, often from a fear of being unable to maintain these relationships. The pastor who leaps from the pedestal seldom realizes the goal of avoiding pain. Too often he or she lands in a pool of crocodiles.

Nothing is less acceptable to a congregation than seeing before them a vivid portrayal of their own potential for unacceptable behavior. This is compounded when the portrayer has held the office upon which they have focused so many of their idealized notions.

If the pastor engages in unacceptable behavior and does not leap voluntarily, he or she is likely to be kicked off the pedestal. Conservative social standards are reserved for clergy, it seems. Divorce, for instance, though widely accepted in contemporary American culture, can threaten a pastor's whole career.

A multitude of pastors have demonstrated that through growth in personal identity and careful nurturing of the potential of the congregation to grow in understanding, it is possible to step down from the pedestal with dignity and lead the congregation in a realistic Christian ministry. Clearer personal and professional sense of identity is vital in the process of becoming a confident pastor. A real person is needed for implementing a call to Christian ministry.

Ministers are individuals and are obviously quite different from one another in their combinations of personality traits. But a number of studies, many based upon the Minnesota Multiphasic Personality Inventory (MMPI), suggest that there are some bedrock likenesses also. The MMPI was another of the measures I used in my work with the three hundred clients mentioned earlier. When the interpretations were returned from the psychiatric institute which scored and interpreted the tests, one identical paragraph appeared in the vast majority: "He appears to be an idealistic, inner-directed person, who may be seen as , quite socially perceptive and sensitive to interpersonal interactions, and may reflect such characteristics as self-awareness, concern for social issues, and an ability to communicate clearly and effectively. He is likely to be sensitive and relatively passive."

The tendency toward idealism and inner-directedness seem a requisite for hearing and heeding a call to ministry. Social perception, sensitivity to interpersonal interactions, and an ability to communicate ideas clearly are basic tools of performance in ministry. The sensitive and sympathetic qualities can be the basis for a nurturing function in ministry if they are kept in perspective. The relative passivity may keep the boat from rocking in some conflict situations but generally can be a harbinger of personal discomfort. It can be an indicator of being overcontrolled.

Clergy seldom have any more hostility than others in a general population, but they tend to fear and keep a lid on what they have. If they do not find a way to express this hostility in a controlled way, their anger or hurt can be turned upon themselves. The result is likely to be depression. On the other hand, they simply explode if the pressure builds beyond endurance. Hostility can also be expressed in procrastination or stubbornness, usually accompanied by guilt.

When basic traits become too pronounced, they become handicaps. But when these same traits are used in positive and constructive ways, they are assets.

Seizing an opportunity for discovering more about who we are and uncovering an inkling of how we use ourselves with others takes courage. By avoiding some of the defenses which impair relationships and by being honest about limitations and abilities, the pastor will go a long way to diminish the pedestal effect. Then the pastor can truly be in touch with those he or she serves.

A real assessment of personal makeup and traits is not done easily by oneself. A supportive and trusted peer group can render assistance. When emotional functioning begins to interfere with relationships and professional efficiency, the assistance of a professional counselor can bring insight and growth. The growth of career-counseling centers for clergy has been very helpful. Centers are within reach of most pastors.

During the past decade many denominations have made efforts to increase the sense of professionalism among their clergy by organizing them into unionlike groups. Members have produced codes of ethics to guide behavior. These groups have also developed a greater voice in influencing their ecclesiastical leadership. As an occupational pressure group, their efforts may occasionally have been successful. But they have produced seemingly scant change in helping ministers establish a sense of identity.

The congregation hires its pastor to assume leadership in most aspects of its functioning. This is what constitutes his or her occupation, and that makes it an unusual occupation. The pastor, like other professionals, chooses the profession out of personal convictions and motivations. Yet in the minister's case there is the added dimension of a call from beyond the self. This is a basic source of identity where self-image merges with role-image. Yet it is a factor of identity which needs more attention from both pastors and congregations. Occupations may differ, but the truth is that the New Testament strongly indicates that the laity and clergy alike are called to be "priests of Christ in the service of God's gospel."

Through the centuries it has been convenient and comforting for parishioners to minimize this expectation in themselves and relegate spiritual activity and leadership to the hired help. Actually, the basic commitment of both pastor and people is to Jesus Christ as Lord of life. All Christians share it. The minister specializes in instructing and leading the community of Christians but has no more need to wear a halo and stand on a pedestal than any other member.

When the pastor and the people recognize this, the way is

opened for the halo and pedestal to be discarded. And that allows the pastor to use the "gifts within," the personal traits, abilities, training, and experience to walk *with* the people. Then they will serve their Lord together.

Perhaps the most provocative thing about the six pastoral roles described in chapter 2 was not what ended up on the list but what didn't. Contrary to expectations, counseling did not emerge as a separate role. Pastors rated the various counseling tasks as being very important, but few said they see it as a separate activity. They distributed these tasks among several roles. We asked Granger Westberg to help us understand why pastors responded this way. His response on the following pages not only points to a logical set of reasons but suggests that behind these reasons is an understanding of the ministry which he finds very healthy. What we end up with here is a view of the counseling function which is different from the way that many pastors were taught in seminary. The standard for counseling may no longer be the formal sessions in the pastor's study, but the conversation following a meeting or on a street corner. Some of the pastors who are frustrated that no one comes to them for counseling may actually be doing the best job of counseling.—*Editor*

7

A Different Look at Pastoral Counseling

GRANGER WESTBERG

When young men and women are ordained and sent out into the big world to minister, there is little doubt that they recognize counseling as a vital part of ministry. Counseling courses, Clinical Pastoral Education (CPE) experiences, and the frequent words of classmates to the effect that they are going to "emphasize counseling" in their ministries all contribute to the notion that counseling is an important pastoral activity.

Yet something happens between the "this is what I'm going to do" stage and the "this is what I've been doing" stage. Pastors in the field reveal that they don't see themselves as formal counselors. Though they recognize counseling as necessary, few pastors actually end up seeing it as a separate activity. They include counseling activities in a variety of pastoral roles rather than seeing it as a role unto itself. In short, pastors see themselves as "informal counseling units."

These are perceptions with which I concur, based upon many years of contact with parish pastors. I would like to list a few reasons why pastors seldom want to be described as pastoral counselors. Let me put it in their own words.

I don't feel expert enough in the field of counseling to hold myself up as one.

I have had so few successes with helping people who were in deep trouble; I see myself as a poor person to be referred to as a counselor.

I can understand why pastors (and family doctors, for that matter) don't want to do that much formal counseling. It is so terribly time-consuming; good results are seldom seen quickly;

there's a feeling of inadequacy because our usual "take charge" approach has to be changed to one of listening and reflecting; and many of us just seem to have a different kind of personality from what is required to really do counseling properly.

I know many pastors, though, who would likely agree with a statement like this one: "I feel good just having brief pastoral kinds of conversations with people on a variety of subjects. I think that once in a while I help someone, and I am often surprised when they tell me how a brief conversation helped them. Sometimes they remember it for years."

But if a parishioner says, "I need counseling, and instead of going to a psychologist, I'd like to see you once or twice a week," the pastor may freeze up and find all kinds of excuses why he or she can't do it.

Those who resemble this pastor may want to try to think of ways to respond to people who want to look to us as formal counselors. Could the pastor, for instance, say, "Thanks for the confidence you place in me, but I am just not cut out for long-term counseling—I'd be glad to see you three or four times to discover what we can accomplish in that time"?

It is essential that we be very forthright with parishioners, promise them nothing more than we can deliver, and then be firm in sticking to what we say we can or cannot do.

Another way to approach such a parishioner is "I'll be glad to try to help you find a counselor who can see you over a long period of time, and then occasionally you can drop into my office for informal talks about anything you want."

It may be that you as a parish pastor *do* feel competent counseling *certain* kinds of problems which people bring. Perhaps this could be stated up front in a clear, precise way, such as "I have no ability in the area of alcoholic or drug counseling. Let me suggest someone who does a really good job along those lines." Or "I feel somewhat competent helping people with normal marriage problems, but when there is a long history of psychiatric problems, I turn these over to special counselors who are better trained than I." Or "I'm a family pastor, which is like being a family doctor. That is, I do my best work with people in early stages of trouble. I'll be glad to try to help you with some smaller problems. In one or two sessions, we can identify a few of those and can probably do something about them."

Pastors spend a good part of their time in conversations with people. Would that be the same as saying that pastors are counselors?

Generally, the name *counselor* implies somebody who is a professional dealing with people who are in trouble. The counselor frequently acts in the role of doctor, psychiatrist, or psychologist giving advice or listening in ways that are appropriate to training in psychotherapy. Further, this is usually a paid relationship which goes on for weeks and weeks and sometimes months and years. Should pastors therefore ever be called *counselors?*

I think it is all right to speak of pastors as counselors provided we know that there are all different levels of counseling. It is easy to conceive of a person with a small problem hailing his minister on the street or meeting him off to the side during a social event. A five- or ten-minute discussion clarifies the problem, and the person is helped.

At other times it might be more formal, and the person may make an appointment to come in to talk, and this may extend on to two, three, or more sessions. This is quite typical for ministers.

Ministers are unique counselors because they are mingling with people constantly throughout the week and are seen as people who will give a ready ear to anyone who wants to talk. What seems like a very unprofessional counseling relationship may actually accomplish more in five to ten minutes than many longer, formal relationships. And much of this is due to the fact that people who look to ministers for help place their confidence in spiritual leaders. A tremendous moral weight is placed on everything that they say. To these persons pastors represent the church, which represents God. Further, because the discussion often happens in the church building itself, an aura of divine third-party participation is often lent to dealing with the problem.

The pastors I have known who are seen by their people as excellent counselors are often men and women who actually do not see themselves as counselors. If they were to describe themselves, they would say that their capabilities lie particularly in the areas of preaching, teaching, and relating to people in a variety of situations. It is this "relating to people in a variety of situations" which makes for a good counselor. While the problems that people want to talk about may be very large or deep at their roots, most people cannot handle the whole problem at once anyway and must deal with it in bits and pieces. And because they were able to take a small piece and deal with it with some effectiveness, they gain more courage to take other pieces and work with them. Just the minister's personal concern and willingness to follow up with further brief conversations encourages the person to assume more responsibility for making certain smaller changes in his life which need to be made before the problem can be solved. But the person does not see himself as a sick person who has to go to a doctor/counselor. Rather, he is a normal, healthy person who is leading an active life and who needs from time to time to discuss certain fairly complex problems with a trustworthy friend.

The fact that pastors spend a good deal of their time in a teaching ministry leads to their being short-term counselors. Some people will participate in a class with a minister for several weeks and get to know this minister very well. If they like what they hear, and they sense that he or she is a sensitive, sensible person, it is logical for them, during the coffee breaks and at odd moments, to discuss things with the pastor. And it is not at all uncommon for them to want to have a private discussion sometime after the course is over. Ministers may not see this as a counseling relationship, but rather as a teaching relationship. Good teachers are often good counselors. Pupils find that it's very easy to talk with a trusted teacher.

Something of the same nature is true of patients who go to doctors to discuss problems which are not strictly medical in nature. We now know that at least half of the patients who go to a primary-care physician have problems that are not strictly physical. In fact, many doctors say that perhaps 50 percent or even 75 percent of their patients have problems that are more in a minister's area of competence than in a doctor's. And yet these people go to the doctor, because in our society it's OK to say, "I'm going to the doctor about my headaches," even though the patient knows there are nonmedical dimensions to the headaches.

It is much the same in people's relationships with ministers. It is perfectly all right to take a course from a minister and then to say that you'd like some further help on some questions which have grown out of the course. It's in those kinds of conferences, which seem to be very much in the teacher-pupil style, that counseling takes place.

In a way, what I may be saying is that the title of this chapter could just as well be "The Pastor as Counselor/Teacher." Good counseling requires that you deal with objective reality and that you have specific problems to look at in some detail. In a similar way, good teaching requires that you have objective facts that must be understood and dealt with as something worthy of learning or getting excited about. The best teacher does not preach or lecture at students but seeks to give small bits of information, then get student reactions to this material to see exactly where the students are and how much they can handle at a time. The good counselor certainly doesn't preach at people, but deals with bits and pieces of the problem and listens carefully to the responses of the counselee, to learn where he or she is in the process of working through these problems.

Have we developed a parish pastor's style of counseling? How does it differ from clergy who have given up the parish and are now full-time professional counselors?

Usually, full-time professional pastoral counselors have chosen to move away from the parish because they feel their talents lie particularly in the area of pastoral care, and so they decide to spend full time in the pursuit of what they feel they do best. Hundreds of pastors have chosen to do this and are working hard at dealing with people whose problems require many, many hours of expert counseling and who would not respond to the usual few minutes or few hours that the average parish pastor is able to give. These pastoral counselors have a real sense of accomplishment now that they have given themselves wholly to such in-depth relationships with people.

Not everyone who goes into the ministry, though, feels called to work at counseling in such depth. If some five hundred clergy in America have decided to do this, we must remember that there are perhaps another three hundred thousand who have decided not to. Of the three hundred thousand, I am guessing that one-third, or about a hundred thousand, of them have real ability along the line of pastoral conversations with people. Although most of them do not have specialized training, they are constantly engaging in helpful conversations with their members and with people who come to them from outside their own parish. This must not be seen as second-rate counseling any more than the work of a general practice physician is of lesser quality than the work of a specialist who works only with a particular part of the body. Each is necessary. People don't need the specialists nearly as often as they need the generalists. This is certainly true within the life of the Christian church. Most people can be helped by brief conversations, by small moments of intensive encounter.

There are five different styles of counseling. For these suggestions I am indebted to the Reverend Howard J. Clinebell, Jr., who is professor of pastoral counseling at Claremont Theological School in California. He believes that there are basic types of pastoral counseling and that if we understand the different types, each of us can choose the ones where we feel most comfortable or choose to use all of them as they seem appropriate for particular people at particular times.

It would be good for us to look at the uniqueness of the pastor's role as counselor. As a representative of a congregation of people, a community of faith, the pastor as counselor sees people long before other counselors. Because of relationships developed over a period of years of ministry, the pastor can often pick things up even before they happen. The one area of expertise which is most helpful to clergy is to understand the early stages of illness: the early stages of grief and loss, the

100

symptoms that arise when people are on their way to getting sick or upset because of changes in relationship in their marriage or between themselves and their children, and so forth. No other counselor has the advantage of such a relationship during the early stages of illness. Normally, a person meets a counselor only after the fact.

Further, the minister is not there just in his or her own right. As a representative of the Christian community and ultimately of God, what the minister says is symbolized by the office. This can carry tremendous weight and value compared to the words of a secular counselor who has merely been recommended as a person who has ability as a counselor.

Ministers are in a position to identify problems in their earliest stages, and they have the advantage of being able to move out toward people. A person's relationship with the pastor is much deeper and perhaps healthier than one with a secular counselor because the pastor is seen as a friend, one who shares with the people their joys as well as their troubles. Ministers can actually knock on the doors of homes of families where they think their presence might be helpful. People wouldn't know what to make of another professional doing such a thing. But when the minister decides to see a family because of problems, it is a simple matter to arrange a house call as a part of an overall visitation of members. The pastor sets aside an hour or two to be with that family informally in their living room where there is an opportunity to sense the threads of relationship between the members of that family.

The minister often has members of the congregation who assist in a variety of ways. Some alert the pastor to people who are at an early stage of a problem. The minister is able to deal with the problem while it is more malleable. Other members have natural gifts as warm, friendly, trustworthy people, and can assist in working with certain other people. In addition, the pastor knows that one, two, or three conversations may need to be buttressed by further discussion and can advise counselees to participate in seminars or discussion groups which may be available in the church or in the community at large. In this way,

counseling or pastoral conversations are integrated with an educational process. These additional supports help to solidify concepts and determinations to make the necessary changes in one's way of life.

PASTORAL CONVERSATIONS

I have chosen to use this nontechnical term simply because I believe that we all are engaged in conversations from time to time which have counseling dimensions. It might even be possible to rank them from superficial on down to depth conversations. It is our hope that seminaries will be able to assist young clergy to learn how to take a superficial conversation and deepen it into one that is more meaningful.

"Pastoral conversations" could carry this deeper meaning if we understand that when a pastor spends time talking with people, he or she is not simply passing the time of day. That doesn't mean that there is always some serious problem, but that when speaking with people, the pastor listens deeply to catch overtones of concerns which they may have. Pastors are particularly able in the area of preventive medicine—in the area of health education. Their desire is to keep people well.

The Sunday worship service helps to serve this purpose. One of the purposes of worship is to give us a weekly chance to take all of our problems and woes into this house of healing and there, in the presence of God, to look at them, knowing that he has invited us to do so. We do not have to carry them alone. People in other helping professions would like their patients and clients to have support groups, which are available to the pastor through the church as a community of potentially concerned Christians. In other words, pastoral conversations are always carried on in the context of a community of faith and are not just two individuals talking with one another.

It is terribly important for people to feel accepted by a group. Personal counseling separated from the world of other people does not have the potential for helping as does counseling done within a community of faith where other people are available.

The pastor is fortunate not to have to carry alone the burden of each person's problems.

In addition to being the leader of a congregation, the minister brings to his or her caring for people all the strengths which come from the heritage of the Christian faith including the Scriptures, the sacraments, prayer, hymns, liturgy, the church building itself. All of these combine to create an aura of relatedness to more than just the present moment of existence.

A friend of mine who was the founder of much of pastoral counseling, Anton T. Boisen, described the minister's helping ability in a beautiful way in his book called *The Exploration of the Inner World.* Let me conclude with his remarks.

> The priest or minister at his best brings to the task of helping the distressed in mind certain insights. He is versed in the utterances of the great and noble of the race, has traced the adventures of the human spirit, both individually and collectively, in its quest of the more abundant life. He understands the deep longing of the human heart and the significance of the constructive forces which are manifest alike in the religious conversion experience. . . . He recognizes the fundamental need of love, the dark despair of guilt and estrangement from those we love, and the meaning of forgiveness through faith in the love that rules the universe and in Whose eyes no one is condemned who is in the process of becoming better. In such insights lie the important contribution of the competent minister of religion rather than in any particular techniques.[5]

Some parts of the parish ministry are considerably more frustrating and guilt-producing than others. Standing at or near the top of the list for many pastors is the teaching role—particularly teaching junior-high-age youth. The Growth in Ministry Project confirmed this, as pastors stated that teaching was a very important part of their ministries. Yet as they rated their effectiveness as teachers, their responses were ambiguous and uncertain. How can you tell if you are accomplishing anything if you spend half of a confirmation-class period keeping Sam from picking on Sally? Peter Steinke meets this frustration head-on in the following pages. He begins by challenging pastors to think about what they are really up to when they face a class. He goes on to say that the teaching models offered in seminaries are the very models certain to fail with a class of junior highs. He concludes with suggestions which can be both liberating and practical. It is easy to see from his chapter that Peter is convinced of the importance of the teaching role for clergy. His enthusiasm is contagious. He just about makes the reader want to run out and gather up a group of junior highs to teach—just about.—*Editor*

8

Pastor as Teacher

PETER STEINKE

The pastor is a teacher. In a wide sense, the pastor is always teaching: conveying facts, sharing feelings, modeling behavior, interpreting symbols, using logic and persuasion, counseling the searcher, expediting group cohesiveness, developing personal relationships, and structuring an environment. We could call this the *wholistic* view—that is, the entire life of the congregation becomes the educational focus. To say "the pastor as teacher" is to isolate teaching, however, as a special task, one among many other roles. It gives attention to formal situations in which there is a consciousness of the task, such as Bible study, leadership training courses, confirmation instruction, and skill-development classes. We could refer to the formal, traditional, and expected educational duties of the pastor as the *particularistic* viewpoint, which is the primary perspective for this chapter.

The Growth in Ministry study, reporting on the pastor as teacher, says in conclusion, "The whole role of the pastor as educator needs serious study." The reason for this summary statement is the finding that while pastors rate the task of teaching to be important, they are at the same time unable to measure the effectiveness of their teaching. If a task is deemed important yet cannot be gauged as to its adequacy, we can expect feelings of demoralizing frustration, diffusion of effort, nagging hostility toward the task, or a loss of purpose. To Lewis Carroll's words— "That's the reason they're called lessons: because they lessen from day to day"—the pastors who participated in the study would have nodded in assent. Let it be put in another context. Imagine a public-school teacher telling you that he or she feels what is happening in your child's class is important, but as yet there is no way to tell if it is in any way effective. Even more, imagine yourself at a physician's office complaining about chest pains, cramps, and nausea, then hearing the doctor say, "Well, what we do here is important, but we have no idea whether or not it is very helpful." To be sure, what the pastors in the Growth in Ministry study have revealed is probably never verbalized in such a manner to their congregations. Nevertheless, the problem is recognized and felt. We can assume that it is still communicated in some way.

But why are pastors unable to evaluate the effectiveness of a task that both they and lay people regard as important? Are pastors actually as ineffective as they suppose themselves to be? If so, what are some of the possible reasons for this state of affairs? Can effectiveness be recognized and achieved? How? Since the study provides no documentation for the causes, these questions will be investigated through some impressions, assumptions, hunches, and observations.

WHAT'S WRONG?

When the dilemmas of the contemporary pastor are raised and debated, the seminaries become typical scapegoats. It is similar to that section of psychology which berates the cold, unloving mother of a psychotic patient or the sociologist who cites the early environment of deprivation in the case of a juvenile delinquent. The period of formation becomes central in explaining current malaise. As significant as the incubating, weaning, and shaping times may be, when the ministry is discussed, something more than fragile youth is encountered. Seminaries are composed of students with maturity. The lack of effectiveness cannot be placed solely at the gates of the seminary. Some apples have to be placed in other baskets, including the pastor's. The pastor is equally a disciple (a trainee) as much as an apostle (a trainer). Neglect of continuing education on the part of the pastor may be a major contributory factor.

But related to both the seminary experience and the pastor's ongoing training is a third feature which makes the entire predicament a drab cycle. How many congregations are eagerly seeking pastors who are adept and skillful pedagogues? The local parish obviously prefers the fund raiser, the preacher, the Pied Piper for youth, the organizer, the go-getter, and the "magic helper." Then too, the church at large rewards these types in their publications and in their assignments. Consequently the two images of the ministry most advertised and emulated are the developer/organizer and the counselor/helper. These are predicated on models from the worlds of business and therapy. The educator model falls lower on the scale of priorities. Consider, for example, how few parish pastors are noted for their teaching competencies. The teacher/trainer role may well be *considered* to be important, but the proof of the pudding is the pastors who feel ineffective.

In summary, we have a three-sided difficulty: the training (seminary), the professional teacher (pastor), and the educational environment (congregation). They intertwine. To help the pastor as teacher, both in terms of self-awareness and in actual practice, to become more effective, the problem needs attention from each of the three sides.

SEMINARY TRAINING

While seminaries cannot be the perennial whipping boys, they more than likely are part of the problem. In my own experience at seminary, for instance, there was one required course in "education," and the paramount (almost exclusive) method of teaching was the class lecture. The same experience is reiterated by colleagues from various age-groups and theological schools.

Out of the Growth in Ministry study, a series of workshops has been developed for Lutheran pastors, appropriately called "The Pastor as Teacher." The response from participants has been overwhelmingly favorable and indicative that many pastors are learning *new* skills and discovering *fresh* insights concerning the educational process. This adds credence to the assumption that earlier seminary training had been sketchy, uninspiring, or inadequate for them.

No doubt seminaries anticipate that a student will upgrade teaching effectiveness during a year of internship or vicarage in a local congregation. But consider this anomaly. In many cases the student will be assigned classes which the supervising pastor does not wish to teach. It may even be enacted in the context of freeing the supervising pastor for other roles of greater import. Rarely, moreover, will the supervising pastor observe the student in practice. It is doubtful that even educators within the congregation's membership are utilized for evaluating the student's teaching effectiveness. It would not be too farfetched, therefore, to suggest that most students graduate without ever having been evaluated in teacher effectiveness through any formal, systematic, or meaningful approach.

Perhaps a greater defect in training students to become pastors who are educators is their encountering of the repetitious methodology of the seminary lecture. It is basically unilateral, moving from the strong to the weak, from the expert to the novice, and from the informed to the unshaped. If the medium is the message, the seminary may be perpetuating, however unwittingly, a cadre of gnostics possessing secret knowledge. Certainly if students mimic the seminary style of teaching later in the parish, they will assume the role of expert. Gradually some pastors realize, though, that they do not have to locate the solutions to myriad problems and questions as a distinctive aspect of their profession, especially in the role of the teacher. At the same time, however, they are at a loss for assessing their teaching effectiveness because the one-dimensional standard of the answer man no longer holds sweeping reign. With the realization that education is not a tool for control, an instrument solely for keeping the flock in the fold, or a unilateral process, what becomes the criterion for judging effectiveness?

Since education is ongoing growth, involving discovery, experience, risk, creativity, emotion, failure, question, and personal interfacing, it is a long jump from being a proficient philosopher to becoming a guide and fellow pilgrim. Hence it appears that seminaries must be as concerned with teaching and modeling skills of communicating, facilitating, interpersonal relating, and interpreting as they are with disseminating knowledge. The *what* and the *how* need a courtship and eventual marriage in these formative years. Otherwise the deceptive image of the pastor as powerful magician who answers or solves the problems of victims or the uninformed will stubbornly persist.

The seminary could play an even more significant role if one of my hunches is correct. I think that teaching skills are best learned *after* there has been some experience in the educational process. Even though a seminary might offer and require additional education courses, alter the one-sided methodology approach, or enhance field experiences with better supervision, this would not automatically increase teaching effectiveness. If the hunch is plausible, the seminaries could offer pastors opportunities in which to evaluate their teaching styles and their effectiveness. This would offer to experienced teacher/pastors a way to build on their experiences. This is simply a restatement of what traditional societies have seen—that life is a school and a teaching force. The effectiveness of the pastor as teacher can be initiated or regained through the particularities of experience and context and a period of reflection on both.

THE PASTOR

The Jews have been very deliberate in the training of their religious leaders. Rabbis are teachers. In the Christian churches there has been an evolution of the role of the clergy from worship leader in the early centuries to the pastor/administrator in the modern day. The role of the ministry has had numerous images: elder, bishop, apostle, disciple, evangelist, servant, priest, teacher, prophet, liturgist, and steward. Unlike the Jewish tradition, pastors in the Christian church are not necessarily or self-consciously prepared to be teachers. Rather, education becomes one of several services offered to the congregation. If it is valid to say that people tend to gravitate toward those tasks which they like to do or which they do well, the task of teaching becomes subject to the same rubric. Pastors can move to areas of enjoyment and skills, which may or may not include teaching. Although a certain amount of teaching must be carried out due to the expectation and tradition of a congregation, nevertheless teaching beyond this point is optional. Since the pastors in the sample study consider their teaching ineffective, are they teaching less and enjoying the ministry more? Or is a latent frustration finally being asserted demonstrably with the hope of help to come? Is the burden, moreover, one with which pastors learn to live as part of the territory, tolerating it because they are successful in other areas? Any one of these cases is likely and possible.

I would like to address the pastor, however, who wants to be a "rabbi," and a more effective one. To do this I will pay attention to one of the most frustrating areas of teaching for Lutheran pastors—confirmation instruction (the early adolescent, twelve-to-sixteen-year-olds)—and to three major ideas about what education entails; in other words, some aids for more adequate teaching.

If teaching ineffectiveness shows up or is felt more often, it most assuredly centers around the confirmation class. Congregations expect pastors to teach the young. If any educational program in the church is inflated with significance, it is the instruction leading to "confirmed" or "communicant" membership for young people. It also stands mainly as the pastor's responsibility. This may sound facetious, but even if the pastor's roles were to be assumed more and more by lay people, Lutheran pastors would still be ordained and called for the "one thing needful" of Lutheranism—confirmation class. In most instances it is the pivot of Lutheran education.

Historically, confirmation arose as a church practice to instruct the baptized in the rudiments of the Christian faith and to provide a public confession of faith in the Triune God in whose name and into whose community they were baptized. This culminated in a public rite. The traditional text for instruction was Luther's *Small Catechism,* written according to the prevalent scholastic method of questions and answers. But Luther's original purpose for the text was bent and distorted. In *Confirmation and First Communion,* Frank W. Klos writes:

> [Luther] wanted to find some ways of encouraging people to probe the teachings of the church on their own and to apply the insights gained to their own lives—and situations. . . .
>
> The fact of the matter is that Luther addressed *The Small Catechism* to the landed farmer, the steady city burgher, to all heads of households whom he held responsible for educating their children and their servants. . . .
>
> Contrary to the way *The Small Catechism* is often used today (like a computer mechanically punching out sterile bits of information), Luther wanted it used as an opportunity for dialogue, exploring the meanings and the ramifications of Christian teachings for each person in his own situation. Further, Luther planned his catechism for use by the whole Christian community, not only children but older youth and adults. . . .
>
> If there is a special use for the catechism in preparing the child for his first communion (and Luther felt there was), it should also be used for the rest of that child's life, guiding him in his growth toward Christian maturity.[6]

What happened, though, is that the catechism received attention almost exclusively in confirmation class. It was relegated to two or three years of study for emerging adolescents; it was not a dialogue starter for relating faith to life but a monologue of doctrines or a small book put to memorization. Above all, this *summum bonum* was placed in the "safe" hands of the pastor. Oddly, lay people could teach the sacred Scriptures but for some strange, mysterious reason the catechetical instruction rested solely with the pastor. The catechism became a quasi-sacred text which the true gnostic in the congregation could alone teach, uncovering its secrets and truths. And yet the catechism would in no way be difficult for high-school or college graduates to comprehend and explain. So today confirmation is "holy ground" where pastors take off their shoes, roll up their sleeves, and feel their hearts burning with frustration. Consequently, confirmation is less a churchly rite and more the pastor's show.

The congregation has gilded the whole affair. A good number of parents, to state it colloquially, still consider that to "get religion" their children must "get baptized," "get confirmed," and "get communion." Although confirmation is not a sacrament in Lutheran terms, it may be merely a step away in too many minds. Luther addressed this problem long ago, calling confirmation "monkey business" because some regarded it as adding to the gifts of holy baptism. Confirmation as recently and currently practiced is far out of proportion to its real significance. To demystify it will take time, because parents do little religious training at home and realize the intense pressures of the secular world on youth. Thus confirmation is the last stronghold, perhaps the only "magic" left for churches to "hold on to the youth." Parents will suffer, therefore, their offspring's complaints, for they know "this is it" in Christian education.

While the congregation in general and parents in particular may expect too much to happen, the students are another matter. They may openly express boredom, hostility, and resistance to learning; they may act it out behaviorally. In turn, pastors may feel threatened. Or other students may accept the bench-bound, sponging arrangement and play the game according to the adults' wishes and rules. This posture of acquiescence leaves the pastor with lower feelings of threat but maybe with higher levels of guilt. But culpability proceeds to another uneasiness, the ambiguity of purpose.

It is not the practice itself which is under question. I doubt if it would have persisted through the years due to the law of inertia alone. The crux of the problem is the unrealistic notions concerning its place in the development of the individual's commitment, the life of the congregation, and the role of the pastor. They perpetrate a built-in ineffectiveness.

Earlier I mentioned that there are three items about the educational process which need elaboration and could assist the pastor in becoming a more effective teacher, that is, aside from improving teaching skills and sharpening one's pedagogical techniques. Let me cite them with reference to the period of confirmation instruction.

Henri Nouwen remarks in *Creative Ministry* that teaching is an *alienating* process. Students are directed to the future where the "real" things happen. "This whole process is alienating," he explains, "because neither students nor teachers have been able to express their own individuality or use their regular relationships with each other as a primary source of learning. They have pulled away from their own experiences; they are staring into the horizon expecting something to appear there, while at the same time they have become blind to what is happening right in front of them."[7] The data is presented as if all will become beneficial later in life. Nouwen suggests that such alienation from the present could be changed if personal experiences and relationships would be regarded as valid educational tools and as complements to content sharing. His understanding of education resembles the very one which Luther proposed centuries earlier.

Unfortunately, however, some have mistaken the voices which call for "experiential" or "relational" learning. They envision it as falling into solipsism, or as avoidance of principles and standards, or still yet, as escaping the rigors and discipline of education. Outside of a few proponents, voices like Nouwen do not intend to replace content or make it a secondary feature. The emphasis on experience and relationship is intended to give content firmer footing and concrete grounding. Besides, inductive learning has its own value, discoveries, insight, and creativity, which might otherwise not have emerged through sheer deduction. Experience and relationship offer a chance for ownership of the information, not always available in a unilateral setup. Content receives a context.

One wonders why the church has been so slow to learn what others have discovered and implemented long ago, especially since a cardinal principle of interpretation of the Bible has been to exegete the content (Scripture verses) in the light of its context (the writer's purpose, historical themes, and so forth). This is appropriate when interpreting the Scriptures, yet for some reason or other, it is not when people interpret their Christian lives. For sure, there is an absence of trust in learners and (contrary to lip service) in the power and promise of the Holy Spirit. We experience the just desserts—the prolonging of alienation. How can one be effective in an alienating situation?

The second area of concern in the educational process, which dovetails with the *affective* side just described, is the *cognitive*. Swiss psychologist Jean Piaget, who has studied the development of thinking, offers considerable help. He has discovered that children from the ages of seven to eleven are capable of what he calls "concrete operations." Simply stated, it means a child of this age bracket can think about *things*. Around the age of twelve and extending to fifteen to sixteen, a new mode of thinking starts—"formal operations." The young person can now think about *thoughts*. Adolescents can reason about contrary-to-fact propositions, understand metaphor, construct ideals, and form hypotheses. They recognize that many factors operate at the same time, that some statements have double meanings, and that a host of alternatives exist causing decision making to be a problem. Adolescents' indecisiveness, incidentally, often erupts into quarrelsomeness. They want to know not only where adults stand but also why. And being able to think about thinking, they become self-conscious and introspective, hence they are ever so concerned about the reaction of their peers, which they acutely monitor.

This new cognitive capability combines, furthermore, with additional drastic changes—physical, genital, and emotional. Indeed, early adolescence is a period of rapid transition, and consequently a period of storm and stress. But pastors, relax! A certain degree of ineffectiveness can be anticipated when teaching this age-group. Argumentation is not necessarily a sign of contention with the teacher's authority or the subject matter's validity. Nor should one confuse adolescent restlessness, questioning, or disinterest with disrespect or dislike. The pastor as teacher of early adolescents can become more free by understanding and accepting the quirks of this stage of development. Life is out of joint for them. Caring acceptance can help them more than keeping them in order. There will be some chaos. It is natural.

A last note on cognition: effectiveness can be gained by adjusting the teaching-learning process to a mixture of concrete and formal thinking. Remember that formal thinking is *developing*; it is not yet full-blown. Concrete examples, anecdotes, visual aids, work sheets, exercises, activities, and assignments are necessary for some. They can only handle the data and think about things. Others who may have advanced to formal thinking can be led to search for meanings. This requires thinking about thoughts. Other behavioral traits aside, it's a good bet that the formal thinkers stand out in discussion sessions. This is not a foolproof test, but it is one way to distinguish the two types of thinkers, enabling the teacher to deal with the student according to his or her cognitive development. The group cannot be cognitively homogenized. Effectiveness can be a by-product of realistic expectations of each student.

The third educational issue revolves around *behavioral* objectives. Teaching effectiveness may be minimized by lack of clear purpose. Why are you teaching what you are teaching when you are teaching it? I believe that the teaching-learning process loses effectiveness if the process does not lead to some activity. Does one teach for apathy? Does one teach for the sake of teaching? Does one teach for giving another more information? Does one teach with merely vague hopes for a return in growth? Or does one teach for something to *happen*? Whether a student is a concrete thinker dealing with data or a formal thinker searching for meanings, the data or meaning might not be translated into action, except for going through the public rite of confirmation. This sets us back to the dilemma of confirmation's exaggerated place in Christian education. A good number meet the congregation's requirements and nothing happens thereafter. Who wouldn't feel ineffective?

I have no unquestionable solutions. But somehow youth ministry and adult education must become equally as significant as the rite of passage of confirmation. New expectations may have to arise. Furthermore, meaningful service for the baptized and confirmed can be explored. There are important types of service besides ushering once in awhile, playing for the high-school group's basketball team, or raising money for youth-group projects. Confirmation lacks behavioral objectives. We don't expect much to happen, and we get what we expect. Why should the congregation wait until she's twenty-five and he's thirty before expecting ministry to occur? We need to retrieve confirmation from its cul-de-sac with some creative and exploratory opportunities for those who have been equipped, though only partially, for the work of ministry.

THE CONGREGATION

The church is "holy." Another way to say it is, the church is special. She is God's vessel brimming with his promises. But something gets lost somewhere. The pastor-specialist is considered to be the only full vessel. The ordained one is the bearer of the promise, in whom the people receive vicarious satisfaction. They accept the paling of their own promise in the shadow of "the pastor." Forget the tired comments about the busy pastor. That is not what I'm talking about anyhow. I'm referring to what has happened to the self-consciousness of the congregational membership as to its ministry and its specialness and its cup of promise. Has God broken precedence which he established in the early church and deposited all the gifts of the Spirit in the pastor's vessel?

Pastors can be ineffective teachers for no other reason than the fact that the rest of the community of believers is goofing off and leaving ministry to the expert. Certainly this is not a new phenomenon. What is happening, though, is that as the roles of the pastor reach higher expectations in the minds of the members, the role of the pastor-as-teacher recedes to the background in favor of roles which ensure congregational growth, survival, or maintenance. An executive director is not expected to be wasting time in small groups, in classrooms, or at training sessions. Why let the pastor coach when quarterbacks are scarce? Teaching may be important, but it becomes a luxury, either because of the pastor's priorities or the congregation's expectations. To complicate matters, what lay people could do well in terms of services offered, they excuse themselves from out of false humility or for reasons of the sheep syndrome—"We need a strong leader."

Surely celebrity pastors are in vogue today, highly admired and successful. But that does not say that's right or preferable. All it says is that's what is in vogue. It is not therefore normative. No doubt the New Testament displays a few celebrated servants of the gospel, most noteworthy being Peter, Paul, and John. But their notoriety can be attributed to their role as teacher as much as anything else. More than half of the New Testament is written by them or their friends.

Although Joseph Sittler's book *The Ecology of Faith* was written over fifteen years ago, his description of the pastor-congregation relationship is just as fitting now as then. "A minister has been ordained to an Office," Sittler comments; "he too often ends up running an office." As a result, pastors feel deeply and strongly a sense of "vocational guilt" which arises from the following circumstance:

> It is hard for the minister to maintain a clear vision of who he is when he is so seldom doing what he ought. His self-image of a servant of the gospel has been slowly clarified, carefully matured, informed, and sensitized during years of preparation. . . .
>
> All of this is under constant attrition in the present form of the churches. And thus it comes about that honesty in the fulfillment of the minister's central task is gradually laid aside in favor of sincerity. Sincerity is a term a man uses to enable himself to live with himself when he has uneasy questions about his honesty. There remain, however, deep down but insistent, voices and remembrances that tell the man what is going on, tell him that the exchange is not a good one. And the enthusiastic readiness of parish and church to accept, even to applaud, the shift makes the suffering of the minister the more acute.[8]

If Sittler's observation is accurate, pastors' "guilt-begetting busy-ness" curtails effectiveness in all roles. Under the current arrangement of the modern pastorate, however, it is my hunch that this becomes most critical in the role of pastor as teacher. Education is a slow process, showing few immediate tangibles, and not an area in which pastors receive reinforcement in any significant or consistent manner. Since people tend to repeat behaviors for which they are rewarded, the pastor as teacher will not gain a balance of *importance* with *effectiveness* under the conditions, priorities, and expectations which prevail in the parish. "Most ministers," Sittler concludes, "are aware that it is a tough and delicate labor to insert the lively power of the Word of God into the rushing occupations and silent monologues of men." How much more true this is if the inserter feels ineffective.

The pastor as teacher, a paradigm lost, can be regained when the seminary-pastor-congregation nexus takes it more seriously and gives thanks that it happens. Effectiveness is related to each of these three variables.

Congregations might be the most helpful by stating more clearly and consciously why teaching is important. Undoubtedly the congregation's purpose for education must transcend the enlightenment of small children and the confirmation experience of youth. Marvin J. Taylor, associate director of the Association of Theological Schools, offers a clue in one of his addresses. He observes that main-line churches have experienced a steady disappearance of the "process of owning the faith in a public way." He continues, "The acceptance of the information from the biblical story is not the same as affirming the validity of that story as 'my faith testimony.'" Too often the church's teaching has been purely privatized, with no other purpose than the obscure goal of "knowing more about the Bible" or "learning about God." How can effectiveness be known when such goals are "ghostly generalities"? Congregations can change their expectations and flatly affirm, teach us for public testimony and (I might add to Marvin Taylor's suggestion) also for public service. Then pastors can say not just "faith makes a difference" but also "here is the difference it makes": it is a personal story of God's love for me in Christ Jesus and an interpersonal story of our loving each other. "Rabbi, teach us . . ."

Sometimes you can learn a great deal about a subject by discovering the things about it which cannot be explained. That would seem to be the case with the Growth in Ministry findings regarding continuing education for pastors. The study disclosed that there is very little correlation between pastors' selection of continuing-education courses and those subjects which they consider important. There was just as little correlation with areas in which they felt effective or ineffective. In short, there seems to be no pattern. We went to Mark Rouch and asked, "Why is there such a haphazard pattern in continuing education?" He responds in this chapter that before continuing-education patterns can make sense, pastors must have a good understanding of what it means to them to be a minister. To some pastors he would suggest that they forget continuing education until other things fall into place. To others he would encourage further study as a part of a "becoming process." His observations are refreshingly put and helpfully reasoned. But the part I like best is where he says, "Have fun."

—Editor

9

Getting Smart about Continuing Education

MARK ROUCH

Recently, in the same city, one week apart, I encountered two men. In those two meetings lies a basic clue to the place of continuing education in life and ministry.

So let me begin by relating the two events, so different from each other.

The first occurred at a consultation on continuing education. As I spoke to the group, one man stood out by virtue of an uneasiness evident in his face and body posture. No sooner had I finished my remarks than he challenged me about a word I had used. It had been, in fact, a poor choice of words, but the challenge had the ring of a quibble over meaning.

The session ended and he joined me quickly as we walked toward the coffee table. The discussion had dealt with some personal issues, and he began at once to talk about the stresses in his personal and professional life. He was pastor, it seemed, of a large congregation. For months he had been without an associate. The congregation expected and demanded many things to which he apparently felt duty-bound to respond.

But something deeper and more pervasive than daily pressures seemed to be at issue. Something in this middle-aged clergyman appeared to be trying to break free but could not, because of the world of external demand in which he lived. Not the least of his longings for a different life was to take more time with his family.

Suddenly I had an image of a human being whose life was being slowly snuffed out by forces which he felt powerless to control.

So I attempted to respond to his lament by asking if there

were not a way he could break free from some of the heavy demands of his job. But my question—or the way I asked it—struck a nerve and I could immediately sense the door shut. His response was that he had from childhood been taught to do his duty; how could he now evade it? It was the voice of a different man from the one who only moments before had tentatively expressed some of the pain of his life.

Soon we parted. How ironic, I thought, that this man, in addition to everything else, should have accepted primary responsibility for continuing education in his judicatory.

Four days later I met another man, and only a few miles from my first encounter. This man, a constitutional historian and a writer on Watergate, was speaking to an assembled group on the state of personal freedom in the United States.

In his opening remarks he spoke of the two fundamental commitments of his life. One was the furtherance of human liberty. The second I report in his own words because they impacted me greatly. He said simply, "I understand myself to be an educator."

Nothing dramatic, certainly, in those words. But when pondered, they are profoundly revealing both of the man's life and of the meaning of vocation.

They first caught my attention that morning because of the way he said them. Communication psychologists speak of statements having "fidelity," by which they mean that when you hear them you know that by diction, tone, cadence they reflect how it really is with the life of the one who speaks.

These words had fidelity. You knew, hearing them, that this man indeed understood himself to be an educator.

Pricking up my ears, I began to reflect upon the words themselves and only then realized what they implied. An educator was what this man sensed—deeply sensed—himself to be. Not an occupation adopted from expedience, not simply a job to earn a living, not an accumulation of atomistic tasks—education was a vocation which sprang from his deepest perceptions of himself. "*I understand myself* to be an educator." Education not only fit him—and how good a fit was evident as he proceeded to *teach* that day—but was rooted in his being, in his self-awareness. "I understand myself *to be an educator.*"

One knew without his saying it that to continue to learn was no burden for this man. Discipline, to be sure, but not burden. Rather, a life of learning flowed from his self-understanding as one might expect water to flow from a spring.

What might I—or you—say to these two men about continuing education? For my part, I would say to the first, "Forget about continuing education. Take *that* burden, at least, from your life. Resign your committee chairmanship. But most of all, release yourself from any personal demand to continue your education. First examine your life and ministry in as much depth as you are willing. See how joy, freedom, and peace can be restored to it."

Of the second I would mainly ask questions: "In what ways do your central life commitments require of you continued learning? In what learning do you find your greatest joy and satisfaction? How do you plan your ongoing education? To what extent does it require discipline? How do you negotiate your choices of time?" And then would come questions and reflections which would grow out of the conversation.

Continuing education, important as it is, is a secondary concern. Primary is the basic flow of life—my life, your life—as human beings and our vocational commitment in dynamic relationship to life. If at the heart of life and vocation something fundamental is amiss, then to concern ourselves with continuing education produces little that is useful; in fact, it may be harmful.

But suppose you or I can say, "I understand myself to be a minister," with the same depth of commitment, the same fidelity that our friend said, "I understand myself to be an educator." In that case the situation changes fundamentally.

If I understand myself to be a minister in that sense, I will experience, first of all, powerful inner motivation to express myself in ministry with the fullest possible effectiveness—including showing forth a genuine humanity. I will also want to respond sensitively and with care to the needs of those about me. I will want skillfully to proclaim the gospel and to teach. In short, from my self-understanding will flow the most basic dynamics which draw one into continuing education for ministry.

Thus the purpose of continuing education for ministry can be plainly stated. *Its purpose is to enable us to engage faithfully in authentic ministry and to do so with effectiveness and satisfaction.*

This, of course, is not to say that continuing education is all that authentic ministry requires. Whether we can accept ourselves; whether we are genuinely open to others and care about them; whether we sense that we are Christ's body in the world; whether we have a lively experience of faith—all of these and more determine what our ministry will be.

Nevertheless, learning is a powerful determinant of authentic ministry. When we keep in touch with what is happening in the world; when we renew and enlarge our knowledge of our faith's tradition; when we have the skills required of our particular type of ministry and acquire new ones; then the competence grows which faithfulness in ministry requires. Otherwise it erodes in unfaithfulness.

But most of you know this already. No use to belabor it. The question for most of us is how we can most effectively link continuing education to the shaping of a more effective and satisfying ministry. To that question we turn now.

But first a surprising fact which has been revealed by the Growth in Ministry study. Perhaps it will not be surprising, because you have seen it in your own experience at times, as I have in mine. It has to do with the way in which the continuing education in which we engage is often not directly correlated with the goals we hold—or profess to hold—for increasing our competence in ministry.

Dr. Thomas Brown said several years ago after a decade of pioneering work in church career-development centers that a large number of those who come through the centers had engaged in continuing education, many of them quite actively. However, there appeared to be an appalling lack of positive correlation between their continuing education and the central problems, hopes, goals of their ministry.

In the Growth in Ministry study, pastors rated their effectiveness in various acts of ministry and the importance of those acts for their ministry. Yet when they indicated areas in which they would like to do further study, there seemed to be little matching with effectiveness and importance factors. In fact, one person who had scrutinized the findings of the study went so far as to suggest that "the pastor's pattern of selecting continuing-education opportunities is often haphazard and not related to the doing of ministry."

There is enough truth in that thesis to make us sit up and take notice. My own experience attests to the growing number of persons who engage in continuing education after careful planning. In far too many instances, however, they appear to engage in continuing education for its own sake, or at least on a hit-or-miss basis without careful attention to how individual episodes or a systematic plan with cumulative effects might shape their ministry.

Even so, my primary intent is not to dwell on the negative instances but to examine the exciting possibilities of ministry being fundamentally shaped by continuing education until as clergy we move toward Timothy's description of "workmen who have no need to be ashamed, rightly handling the word of truth."

In what follows I would like to look with you at the excitement of continuing education having direct effect on how we do ministry, that is, an "immediacy"; then at how planning can have powerful cumulative effects on ministry; and finally, how we can plan effectively.

First, however, let me define what I mean by continuing education so that you will know what I have in mind as we proceed. I will use "continuing education" as a shorthand way of referring to continuing education for ministry unless I indicate I am using it in its broader meaning.

In my book *Competent Ministry: A Guide to Effective Continuing Education* I have developed a full interpretation of continuing education, which I commend to you if you want to probe its meaning.[9] I will not repeat or summarize here what I have written there. But to state the definition which I used will let you know what I have in mind as we proceed.

> Continuing education is an individual's personally designed learning program (developed with the help of colleagues [laity and fellow clergy]) which begins when formal education ends and continues throughout one's career and beyond. An unfolding process, it links together personal study and reflection and participation in organized group events.[10]

The words in parentheses were added by Dr. Connelly Gamble, emphasizing rightly the importance—indeed, the critical importance—of collegiality in one's continuing-education development.

Your life and work provide the ongoing basis, or the "curriculum," of your continuing education. No school, no externally planned program provide the curriculum. It unfolds out of our own life and work, where also it has its nourishing roots.

In the five years since I wrote that definition I have increasingly focused my attention to who we are as the persons whose lives provide the basic continuity of our continuing education.

First, we are human beings whose lives are inextricably woven into a web with the rest of humanity. We cannot, by virtue of that, be individualistic, to say nothing of self-serving, in our continuing education. Not, at least, if we are to be true to the gift of life bestowed upon us in our creation.

Furthermore, we are ministers, in our case clergy, who, whatever else, are called to be servants in Christ's name—not to be confused with being servile. In this we come full circle back to the purpose stated earlier. Our continuing education is to enable us to engage faithfully in authentic ministry and to do so with effectiveness and satisfaction.

Two keys to that happening lie, first, in our experiencing what I would like to call an "immediacy" of effect and, secondly, in experiencing the cumulative results which come from careful planning.

IMMEDIACY

By immediacy of effect I mean an awareness that individual episodes and activities—seminars, workshops, books, study guides

—are having a definite direct and noticeable effect on the quality of life of some part of our ministry.

But let me say what I mean by telling you about Nettie McClure, who lives in Gold Mine, North Carolina.

Mrs. McClure is a master craftswoman in making patchwork quilts. Eighty-two years old now, she can piece any quilt from the Lone Star to Ocean Waves—at least that's what John Parris, who keeps us in touch with mountain folk through his column in the *Asheville Citizen,* told us recently.

Nettie especially likes the Double Wedding Ring, and that's my favorite, too, because my grandma Barnard and great-grandma Campbell made one as a gift when Phyllis and I married.

Nettie never has liked quilting bees very much. Quilting, to her, is personal. She does it because, in her words, "I have to satisfy myself." And her satisfaction is closely related to competence (a word I'm sure she never uses). "The piecing means perfect points and corners and exact shaping of the pattern."

Most intriguing to me is how Nettie McClure learned to quilt. She had watched her mother do it. So when she married, she just started quilting with frames made by her father and patterns from her mother—a self-taught craftswoman whose love for her craft was born with her and formed as she had watched her mother.

But Nettie in those days used no thimble—and needed none, "Thank you!"

Here enters the upsetting educator, her mother-in-law, who said, "Nettie, you'll never sew without a thimble." Nettie would reply, "Yes, I can," and go right on. Not unlike other great educators, Nettie's mother-in-law would not rest content with an inadequate method no matter how functional in its limited way. "She kept on telling me," says Nettie, "that I'd never quilt without a thimble or I'd jab my fingers off. Then she'd tell me what finger to put it on."

So Nettie McClure finally put on the thimble and got to learning how to push the needle through with it. Now, at eighty-two, she looks back over her career: "Law, I couldn't never have sewed without it. I've thought of her a thousand times since then. I've thought, well, I'd never quilted or anything without that thimble. No sir, you can't make a quilt without a thimble."

"No sir, you can't make a quilt without a thimble." That's what I mean by *immediacy*. Learn to use a thimble and *at once* become more effective in making quilts—and more satisfied. Take a speed-reading course and experience session by session increased speed and comprehension. Engage in a preaching workshop with the help of videotape and find that the first Sunday home, three lay people whose judgment you trust tell you how effective your sermon was. Sweat through Wolfhart Pannenberg's *Jesus: God and Man*[11] and experience the new way your mind reflects on Jesus during the Lenten sermon preparation. Learn in a workshop how to develop a family system in marriage counseling and then see insight light up the face of the anxiety-ridden husband in the next counseling session.

You can name your own experience, but they all have the same character: seeing definite, direct results of a learning experience in the practice of our ministry, or in life itself.

When we experience such immediacy several things happen. We want more of the same, for one thing. Education produces results we value, so we want to learn more. This very experience of some simple, direct result has been the doorway through which many persons have entered into lifelong learning.

For another thing, it gives learning itself a fun quality—not ecstatic joy, just plain, ordinary fun. It is pleasurable, after all, to learn something which will produce some results we really want, even more pleasurable when the results occur.

Most important, the quality of our ministry changes, and that, after all, is what we're after. When "I understand myself to be a minister" and see that ministry enhanced, I experience deep satisfaction and know that I am being thereby the more faithful in my calling.

How does such immediacy occur? Occasionally by chance, but not often. Usually it requires knowing what we want to change in ourselves or our ministry. That, as we shall see, is the starting point for continuing education planning—not a random survey of continuing education opportunities. Secondly, it requires that we make a careful choice of the educational resource which will help effect the change we desire. Finally, it is all affected by the frame of mind we bring to the learning experience. If we enter it with curiosity, alive and eager for the search, the chances of significant learning are much higher than if we do so with plodding determination to "get through" one more educational event.

We may also simply follow our curiosity. For example, we may read a book on Disraeli simply because we enjoy biography and are fascinated by Disraeli. Or we may study art simply to feed our souls. Such learning will have its effect upon ministry simply because it enlarges life.

Before we move on to the cumulative effects of planning, I want to qualify what I have said about immediacy—not to detract from it but to put it in its proper perspective.

Not all useful learning will have immediacy. Sometimes we will direct ourselves to a body of knowledge or skill which we know is important but which for the moment produces few noticeable results. But later we find ourselves drawing upon the store of what we have learned. That is true, for example, of much biblical study.

CUMULATIVE EFFECTS

We turn now to the cumulative effects of continuing education when carefully planned.

Valuable as the immediacy effect is, it will not of itself produce significant change in life and ministry over the long haul. That kind of change requires a systematic approach over a period of months or years.

Here is an example of what I mean. Roger finds that more and more families in his church are in crises of one kind or another. Enough of them approach him for counseling so that he knows he has the congregation's basic trust as pastor. Yet some seem to hold back; just why, he is not sure. Roger's experience in counseling sessions tells him that he has gifts which could make him effective in family-crisis counseling. At the same time he knows that in one or two instances he has seriously mishandled a counseling interview. Lately he has heard about the use of family-system theory in counseling, and it has pricked his curiosity.

All of this adds up to the sense that this part of his ministry requires improvement. At the same time it offers exciting challenges. Roger has a friend nearby who spends a good bit of time in counseling, is accredited by two associations, and has a sound reputation as a counselor. So he talks to Helen, who confirms that she does see Roger as having gifts in this area and agrees to read a couple of verbatim reports of his counseling sessions.

Their later conversation about the verbatims leads Roger to attend a short workshop on family-crisis counseling which Helen is conducting in a nearby continuing-education center.

During an extended day a month later, Helen assists Roger, as a paid consultant, to lay out a two-year plan for growth in this area of ministry. The first period involves a reading and tape-listening program for six months while Roger completes another continuing-education project and investigates a nearby clinical pastoral education program heavily oriented to the in-service needs of the pastor. The program appears to meet Roger's need, so he decides to enter it for a one-year period provided he can arrange with his church to take one day each week. He thinks they will agree, since the learning involved will be directly related to their needs.

The second year is left open to several alternatives, depending on the results of the CPE unit. One would be an M.A. at a nearby university (in which case two or three additional years might be required). Another would be several seminars or workshops in which Roger would be exploring his own personal journey as a human being, which he realizes has great bearing on his sensitivity as a counselor.

What a difference between that and continuing education in which randomly one reads a book because the title is intriguing; then goes to a preaching workshop because Fred's going and it's fun to be with him; then uses a study guide with a colleague group with little input on the choice of subject; then goes to a workshop because the leader is famous and it will be interesting to see him in action.

None of these in itself is all that bad. The loss is in the fact that as a rule they add up to very little except a dilettante's self-satisfied enjoyment.

If we "understand ourselves to be in ministry," if we experience ministry as a gift and an offering, if we care about faithfulness and authenticity, then we will want to see continuing, substantial changes occur in our ministry. That will require the seriousness and care in planning which Roger's experience represents.

PLANNING

I turn now to look at how we plan. I do so realizing that many of you already plan your continuing education. If so, I invite you to reflect on what I suggest to see if there are ways to enhance your planning. If you have not yet begun to plan, what I hope to provide are handles to take hold of in order to get under way.

Planning begins with ministry, not education. I hope that has been evident in all I have said. But it needs reemphasis here because so often we start with the question, what kind of continuing education should I—or could I—be doing?

Wrong question. The right question: what is it about my life and ministry that I want to change?

Two sets of variables affect how we answer that question: (1) satisfaction/dissatisfaction and (2) effectiveness/ineffectiveness. Among the various roles of ministry and the particular tasks within them are some which give us satisfaction while others do not—and in varying degrees. Some we carry out effectively, a few with great competence; some ineffectively, a few dreadfully so.

A simple analysis of ministry around these variables is one of the best ways to decide what you would like to change. Let me suggest an experiment which requires only a few minutes. For this I am indebted to Sister Marlene Helpin, a leader in the continuing education for ministry movement.[12]

First, list quickly, brainstorming fashion, every task you perform as a professional minister, all the way from unlocking the church building to liturgical leadership to denominational responsibilities—everything.

Now, since you did it quickly, go back and eliminate overlaps, repetition, and so forth, but do not combine items. For a moment now, let me have the fun of assuming that I have magical power over your life. With that power I will say to you that for the rest of your ministry you can keep only ten of these tasks. Pick them out and mark them. (That, of course, is not a "real life" sort of choice but it does have the "real" value of a forced choice in deciding what matters most.)

Write these ten tasks on a separate sheet of paper and rank them in order of their importance to your ministry. Then rank them according to the amount of time you spend on each.

Next, on a full sheet of paper draw a large diamond with the four points labeled as below.

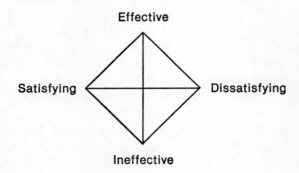

Write each of the ten tasks in one of the quadrants. You may even want to place them within the quadrant at the point which best represents how it is with your performance of that task.

Before you now are useful basic data for building a continuing-education plan. You may see graphically the possibility of building on the strength of a task in the effective/satisfying quadrant. For example, teaching may bring you high satisfaction partially because you know you are good at it: you have seen persons change significantly in classes you have led.

Or you may see that administration, an essential part of being pastor, leaves you cold, and you plod along at best or bungle at worst. It's far down in the lower and right quadrant. But you know that a friend participated recently in a management-for-ministry seminar and has moved this task from where you are now up into the effective/satisfying quadrant. After all, enhancing one's skill in learning to help others utilize their gifts and abilities can be highly satisfying.

This analysis—or something like it—is a beginning but only that, especially if we are committed to the collegiality of ministry. Essential to our planning is to discover how others see the importance or unimportance of these tasks in our particular ministry setting. Secondly, it is important to learn how effective or ineffective we are in them. Their experience of us need not cancel out our own perception, but if we are open, it may modify our own perception significantly.

Information from whom? Our spouse, certainly—and for reasons we know well, this is often the most difficult to accept. We can receive it from our children who see us in ministry—and at home—and have, usually, uninhibited candor.

We need to know how they rank the importance of our central tasks and whether there are some which rank high with them that are not on our list. Most important, we need to know how they evaluate our effectiveness in these tasks and on what basis. When they know how we see our ministry and we know their views (which will usually be highly varied), then we need to negotiate what tasks will rank high in our continuing-education plans—both on their behalf and our own.

Besides family and key members of our congregation or employing agency, it is important to know how professional colleagues who know us well and denominational officials who have a chance to observe our ministry see it and let that information also enter into our planning.

This process of information gathering is the most critical element in our continuing-education planning, yet often the most difficult.

Why is it so difficult to hear—really hear—how others perceive our ministry? The question is the more puzzling because such information is likely to produce many affirmations of our competence.

The key to the answer is in our self-image. Many of us who are ministers have, for whatever reason, low self-image; we have not learned to value ourselves. Hence, when criticized, we say to ourselves, "Yes, they see me as I really am," or when praised, "Don't they know that I do not respect myself? How can they really mean it?"

I have overstated the case. But all of us, I suspect, have had enough inner uneasiness about our self-image to know what a barrier it can be to this step in our continuing-education development.

If we sense that the problem is critical, perhaps the first necessary step in our long-range growth would be to seek counsel to help improve our self-image—which, by the way, with all of its risks, is one of the most satisfying journeys upon which a human being can enter.

If the rather simple analysis I have suggested above intrigues you but does not seem to go far enough, there are resources to help you with a thoroughgoing analysis. *Needs assessment* is the name generally given to the processes and instruments available. They vary widely. Most have workbook materials connected with them; a few require advance tests or inventories which are scored and interpreted during a group workshop. Some are designed for individual use suggesting that others be invited to contribute feedback information; some include evaluation by the congregation; others do not.

If you want further information about these needs-assessment processes, write to the Society for the Advancement of Continuing Education for Ministry for their report of a recent study of them.[13]

Most needs assessment focuses on effectiveness in one's present job. But to plan well-rounded continuing education, you and I also need information about other ongoing aspects of our life and work. Three types of questions need to be asked:

1. *Do I need further work on my self-concept or self-image?* Low self-esteem is not only a block to evaluation, as we have said, but inhibits authentic ministry in many ways—besides making us just plain miserable. Dr. Donald Super, for many years at Columbia University, has said that "a career is an implementation of a self-concept in the world at work." That being true, nothing is more basic to our long-range career development than self-concept.

2. *How is it with my family relationships?* Warm, nourishing relationships contribute remarkably to the vigor and joy with which we invest ourselves in our work, while cold, enervating relationships detract. Thus, again, to work with a spouse or as a total family on this basic part of our lives affects career development. An assessment of how it is with family relationships may provide a clue for a family- or couple-related learning experience.

3. *What about my long-range career future and its development?* Do I intend to stay in this particular job very long? Is a different occupation a possibility? Am I approaching or in a major life or career "passage point"—the early trial stage, midcareer, preretirement? Do I have strengths and abilities which will serve me well for years ahead and which it would be a joy to develop over the long haul? Is there opportunity down the road for an extended study-leave of three to six months, or even a year's sabbatical, if I plan, save, and search for scholarship aid?

All of these questions and others are not unrelated to your present job, but they also transcend it and represent significant data which ought not to be overlooked as we plan.

Once the information—or as much as we need—is in hand, how do we plan? Here also I would refer you to what I have written in *Competent Ministry,* where I have answered this question in detail.

Most of us are aware that educational resources to respond to our needs are vast and growing daily.[14] Let me here offer only a few pointed suggestions.

1. Give major attention to what you can do at home, largely through your own initiative. Wherever else you may turn, your own study is still the primary "schoolroom" of your continuing education. If you are not engaged in it there, what you do elsewhere adds up to little.

Consider what you might do with laity of your congregation as colleagues—studies with them under someone else's leadership, or using tapes or study guides. Colleague groups of other clergy provide not only a basic support relationship but also an arena for education. Study guides and group-oriented cassette tape programs are among the many resources available.

2. When you go to a seminar or workshop away from home, check not only the program content but, just as important, check out the style of the education. For example, does it take you as the learner seriously as a participant in education, drawing upon your insights and taking your questions seriously? This "research" often requires contact with a previous participant.

3. If you are considering a doctor of ministry degree as a method of planned, discplined continuing education, let me suggest the following: First, it is just that—a planned, disciplined process which many find useful as motivation. Secondly, look carefully to see if it takes seriously your own professional practice and is not simply another roughed-over liberal-arts and sciences degree oriented primarily to the academic. (Which is not to depreciate the importance of its being academically respectable.) Finally, does it provide the resources to help you accomplish goals you have set for your own growth in ministry? Far too many have enrolled in the D.Min. degree without clear goals of their own, thinking that it would enhance their professional marketability, only to be disappointed. However, many with clear goals have completed the degree, including in their program projects of major significance for their ministry, with the deep satisfaction of recognizing a quantum leap in competence.

4. This final item is really a parting wish: let your learning be filled with joy. From the earliest studies made of ministers in continuing-education events until now, the rest and relaxation factor has been present. This has always alarmed some serious educators. But I have always found myself impishly rejoicing in it.

Perhaps that is part of my own confession that I enjoy learning for learning's sake. I am a "learning oriented" learner, as Cyril Howle would say. But I see so much education that is boring. I can tolerate its being bad education—the human spirit can survive that. I rejoice when it has excellence. But boring— that is surely of the devil!

So whatever you do on your journey of continuing education, *enjoy it. Rejoice in it. Glory in it!* After all, you are satisfying one of the deepest longings of the human spirit.

Besides all that, have at least one good pizza or steak dinner whenever you attend a seminar. And play a little tennis.

Probably the most neglected part of a pastor's ministry is with his or her own family. There are special needs there, claims Dave Martin. That's not news. In the following pages he uses one couple to illustrate the kinds of pressures that descend upon many clergy families. What's good about this chapter is that parts of that couple's dialogue sounded disturbingly familiar. These made me stop and think. They may have the same effect on you. But Pastor Martin doesn't stop with a description of the problems, he continues with insightful analyses of how these things popped up and how they might be handled constructively. There is grist for the mill here for unmarried clergy as well. The issue is not simply the pressures upon marriage relationships, but upon all close and supportive relationships. Those who are closest to us are often the ones to suffer the most when parish duties demand time and attention. One Growth in Ministry finding which Dave cannot change with these pages is that while most clergy see the importance of marital counseling and enrichment opportunities, very few would participate in them themselves. Perhaps they are afraid that others will see. The pressure to have the perfect family which never has need of help can end up being the very pressure which dooms some families. This would be a good chapter to read and discuss with someone you love.—*Editor*

10

Forgotten Members:
The Pastor's Family

DAVID MARTIN

The issues which face the pastor's marriage and family are as broad and deep as those which affect any marriage and family in these times of changing values. Traditional concepts of marital fidelity and commitment and of the role of men and women in society have been challenged by changing attitudes and contribute greatly to the present-day turmoil in marriage and family. Being set apart, so to speak, to do professional ministry does not insulate pastors, their spouses, and their families from these changing values. But there are some marital and family issues that are unique to the professional person and, for the purpose of our discussion, unique to the pastor. The substance of this chapter is based on portions of the Growth in Ministry research study and my own observations and conclusions. At the time the study was completed, there were so few women pastors that none surfaced in the study's random selection technique. Therefore, the study's frame of reference is families with male pastors and female spouses. I've maintained that perspective in this chapter, yet many of the issues may apply just as well to families in which the wife is the professional pastor.

In order to get into the issues concretely and specifically, I'll share a conversation between Tom and Betty Jones. Tom, thirty-seven, has been in the ministry eleven years and has served one congregation. They were married in seminary, and Betty has taught school since their first year in seminary with the exception of two brief maternity leaves. Tommy, Jr., is three and Susan is eight. Tom is pastor of St. Paul's Church, and he and his family live in the parsonage adjacent to the church's educational wing.

Tom perceives that his ministry at St. Paul's is at a turning point. He could stay for a few more years and develop new goals for his ministry there, but he would prefer to move on to another parish. He has been in conversation with his bishop concerning a new call. The bishop has recommended that his ministry profile be given to the call committee of Bethel Church. Tom has consented. Tom and Betty are in the living room after dinner and the children are outside playing.

Betty: I don't see why you're so intent on pursuing a call to Bethel.

Tom: Betty, it's a good opportunity, and I think I can provide them with the kind of enthusiastic ministry they have been lacking for years . . . and the salary package is much better than what we have now.

(*Silence.*)

Betty: (*discouraged*) I'd just hate to follow Barbara Smith.

Tom: What are you saying, Betty?

Betty: She was just the lifeblood of that congregation . . . into everything. Why . . . she had open houses, taught a Sunday school class . . . she's been president of Bethel Women a number of times . . . organizes all the dinners . . . she's involved in the community. From what I hear, she was a big part of Dr. Smith's ministry. (*silently*) Everybody loved her.

Tom: (*impatiently*) What of it?!

Betty: Oh, Tom! You know that's not me!

Tom: Well, what makes you think you have to be a Barbara Smith?

Betty: It's not that, Tom. It's what they expect after sixteen years of her. (*intensely*) I'm just not ready to do battle with everybody's expectations, and I'm not Barbara Smith! I'm a wife, a mother, a teacher, and a faithful member of the church. . . . I love you, I'll support you, but I won't be the second pastor. (*Tears well up in her eyes.*) God knows how little time we have together now . . .

(*Pause.*)

Tom: The only thing I can say, honey, is that they aren't expecting me to be Dr. Smith, and I doubt seriously if they are expecting you to be another Barbara. (*Pause.*) I didn't think you felt this way.

Betty: But Tom, how many times have we been over this. I just feel like we're living in a fishbowl. Your office is here in the house. When you're with us, you're a step away from your office and the church phone . . . and the little time you have you spend with the children . . . and there's no time for us. (*Tears and sobs.*) We haven't even had a good experience in bed for months.

Tom: Now, Betty. (*placatingly*) Are things really that bad?

Betty: (*barely above a whisper*) N-n-no . . . but they could be better.

(*Betty walks out of the living room to the bathroom. Tom busies himself with sermon preparation.*)

What is most obvious about this exchange between Betty and Tom is Betty's hurt, her feelings of inadequacy and of being neglected. It is also apparent that Tom did not expect the avalanche of feelings from Betty. A number of issues emerge during the course of the conversation. First, Betty is dealing with a rigid, stereotypical image of what a pastor's wife *should* be as she perceives that image to be embodied in Barbara Smith. Along with this, she expresses some guilt over pursuing her own career. Second, her feelings of neglect are a good indication that they have had little time together not only as a family but especially as a husband and wife. Also, she expresses that the little time they have together as a couple is far from satisfying even the most intimate aspects of their life. Third, Betty expresses the way she would like to be perceived as a supporting spouse but struggles with the feeling that it may not be adequate. Fourth, she feels like she is living in a fishbowl, exposed to the congregation and community with little private time for herself, for Tom, and for the family. Fifth, she perceives that there is a confusion of boundaries, both physically and emotionally, between Tom's professional life and their personal life. And finally, Tom and Betty do not know how to cope with their feelings. Both have found ways of withdrawing themselves and their feelings. Perceptions of each other are inaccurate and communication has broken down. Their marriage is in trouble.

Let us look at these issues one at a time and at some possible ways Tom and Betty might deal with them.

THE SPOUSE AND THE MYTH

The myth of the perfect pastor's wife prevails in the minds of many pastors, spouses, and church members. For Betty the myth was embodied in the person of Barbara Smith. It is assumed by many people that the perfect pastor's wife should have a high level of involvement in the parish, assume leadership roles in the women's organizations, possess certain skills and a willingness to share these skills such as organist, teacher, speaker, and organizer. Also, it is expected of the perfect pastor's wife that she possess a high degree of sociability and feel comfortable entertaining in a variety of situations. Further, the myth characterizes the wife as a full-time homemaker with major interests in the church and community, with no particular career aspirations outside of her husband's profession.

The perfect pastor's wife is a myth simply because pastors' wives are unique individuals with their own personality traits, raw and learned skills, personal career directions, and varieties of interests. Some wives may be the types which prefer to live out the perfect pastor's wife image and are comfortably suited in fulfilling the role in varying degrees. Other wives prefer pursuing other interests, with a minimum involvement in the parish.

A number of factors contribute to a changing image of the pastor's wife. The changing roles of men and women in society have challenged traditional male/female roles, and women are involved in a variety of jobs and professions that have been dominated traditionally by men. Doctors, lawyers, institutional administrators, political officials, and businesswomen are found in the ranks of pastors' wives. Another factor is that many pastors' wives now seek employment as families find it necessary to have two incomes due to low salary levels and the shrinking dollar. What is especially significant about the working wife is that many have skills and qualifications gained in college and graduate school which they prefer to use outside of the context of home and parish.

An issue which faces a number of clergy families is that the expectations pastors have of their wives may be in conflict with the wives' expectations of themselves. A perfect illustration of this is the wife who worked during her husband's seminary career, putting him through school, so to speak. After graduation, accepting a call, and ordination, the husband assumed that his wife would not seek further employment and would become a dutiful homemaker with a high involvement in parish life. However, this was not her expectation. It came as a shock to her since he had not made his expectations clear during their seminary experience. This conflict of expectations created much pain in their marriage, and only after extended counseling were they able to work out a solution.

It is essential that the roles, images, and expectations of the pastor's wife be dealt with openly and honestly by the couple. There are a number of creative ways that this can be done. First, it is important that an attempt be made to develop a clear understanding of what each marriage partner expects of the other regarding how the marriage and family relate to the parish. While total agreement on expectations may not be realistic, mutual appreciation and understanding of each other's needs (for example, the wife's fulfillment in a career) is essential to creating harmony in the marriage. Second, interpreting the role of the wife in the parish can be a joint effort which may lead to confronting parishioners' expectations and building a healthy climate of understanding. Pastors and wives have been known to interpret the wife's role in the parish in conversations with call committees in order to create an understanding even prior to entertaining a formal call. Also, throughout their ministry husbands have supported their wives by interpreting the wife's role in the parish along with her. This partnership in interpretation assists the congregation in understanding her role and reduces conflict where hidden assumptions have been exposed.

THE TIME BOMB

Betty has strong feelings that her husband has neglected her and the family. He spends so little time at home. Yet even when he is there, she feels the constant anxiety that he may be called away at any moment to respond to some parish crisis.

Many pastors could be characterized as absentee fathers and husbands, a phenomenon which has been descriptive of many professional men. Evening calls, meetings, and counseling sessions intervene in the life of the family, since there are no clear distinctions such as a nine-to-five workday. The situation is confused even further for pastors who have an office and church phone in the home. Time that he promised to spend with the wife and family is frequently interrupted by emergency situations and unanticipated counseling opportunities. Sermon preparation may be done in the evenings after the phones have stopped ringing. His weekends are filled with parish demands, while his wife is off work and the children are home from school.

The demands placed on the pastor's time by parish responsibilities have effects on the task of rearing children. Consciously or unconsciously, the pastor-father may abdicate the responsibility of rearing and discipling the children to his wife. The pressures of the parish can cause the pastor to be less receptive to the problems and issues at home. If there is no consistency in discipline of the children, new problems may arise as the children receive conflicting signals from the parents. The words "wait till your father gets home" provide little incentive for children to reflect on their own behavior if the father does not follow up in an active parental role. Another family problem can arise if the mother uses the children to manipulate the father. She may try to have the children takes sides with her against the absentee father.

Betty's feelings of neglect may be prompted by the way her husband relates to her as a wife. Research indicates that many pastors relate to their wives and children as a unit, making little distinction between wife and children as they express love and affection. This is partly due to the common concerns and interests the mother has for the children and how she communicates their needs to the husband-father. The wife's individual needs for love and affection become merged and submerged in the children's needs as the husband fails to make distinctions. The reverse is not true, however, as the husband is perceived by the wife as an individual, separate from the children's needs and concerns.

Pastors who place a higher intrinsic value on their work than on the more "mundane" family affairs pose a strong threat to their wives and children. How does the family compete with God? This can be a volatile issue for many wives and children. Their value of the family is in direct conflict with the husband's. The husband's argument can be disarming and very frustrating to his family when he asks, "Don't you expect me to put God first in my life?" But is there not a confusion between God and work in this statement?

That pastor displays his values in his use of time. The statement "I don't spend much time with my family, but it's the quality of time I spend with them that is important to me" is another myth that many people accept without realizing that time has no intrinsic value. The "quality" of any time shared with a wife and children is inevitably a question of the quality of their relationships and how that time is used in nurturing these relationships. That takes time.

There are a number of ways that the issue of time can be dealt with by clergy families. One is to work out mutually agreeable goals for time shared with spouse and time shared with family. The goals must be concrete, realistic, and attainable.

Pastors may protect that time by planning for a back-up person in case of emergencies, emphasizing stated office hours, and clearly communicating to the parish any particular times of the week that are devoted to the family. Family and marriage enrichment retreats and trips out of town with mutually desirable activities for the whole family provide the framework in which a nurturing family operates. There is a final important ingredient. Family members must take their commitments to one another seriously. When a commitment must be broken, the family should discuss it thoroughly and plan alternatives.

SUPPORTING ONE ANOTHER

Betty has a definite feeling of how she supports Tom as she says, "I love you, I support you, but I won't be the second pastor." To Betty, supporting Tom means supporting him as a person rather than supporting him with a high degree of involvement in the parish. Just as there are varying ways that spouses involve themselves in parish life, there are varying ways that they may support their mates. The mythological role of the pastor's wife indicates a high degree of involvement in the parish and is characterized as husband-wife team ministry. But this should not be confused with team ministries in which both persons are ordained. For one wife, support may mean emphasizing a creative and satisfying home experience with a moderate degree of involvement in the parish. For another wife, support may mean active participation in the parish with her husband, even to the extent of making calls on prospective members and visiting the sick and shut-ins with him.

Wives who tend to support their husbands as persons in the home indicate interest in making the husband's personal life fulfilling by creating opportunities for relaxation, renewal, development of mutual interests outside of the parish, a mutually satisfying sexual relationship, and a healthy dose of empathetic understanding. Not that this cannot be done with a variety of responses to parish involvement, but the emphasis is on the home. The pastor whose wife is deeply involved in the parish appreciates her supportive involvement with members he may not feel comfortable in relating to. Wives on both ends of this scale feel strongly about the kind of support they offer. When the partners agree on methods of support, there is satisfaction.

FISHBOWL OR LIMELIGHT

The pastor's family is exposed to a community of parishioners and the surrounding community by virtue of the pastor's position as shepherd of the parish and a community leader. The home or parsonage seems to be accessible to persons for a variety of reasons. Members of a parish who feel close to the pastor, members with problems, and persons off the street may visit uninvited and unannounced. Some persons visit out of curiosity about the pastor's home and family. The situation may be compounded further if the home is a parsonage owned by the church, and then the family may be invaded by a property committee or a well-meaning custodian. People who are curious about the pastor and spouse and children may even know when the family rises and goes to bed, and what's in their garbage can. Some parishioners who have certain expectations of the pastor's family may be interested in the behavior of the family. There are many humorous and heartbreaking stories about the pastor's home. It all adds up to exposure.

Betty perceives this exposure as living in a fishbowl, exposed to parishioners and community. Another spouse may perceive the exposure differently and describe it as more like living in the limelight. What makes the difference is not necessarily the situation but personality. Betty perceives the exposure as negative because of her personality. She is probably more introverted than extroverted. She may have had experiences in her childhood when her privacy was invaded by others, and she has become reactionary to the exposure. Whatever the case, she prefers more privacy than she experiences in the home. Another spouse may characterize this exposure as limelight, where more extrovertive needs and desires are satisfied by opening the doors of the home frequently to parishioners and others.

It is inevitable that every parish pastor's home will have some exposure, but one person's pleasure may be another person's poison. Betty reacted to Mrs. Smith's open house over the holidays because Betty views the home as a more private domain. Pastors who own their own homes may be less susceptible to this exposure, especially if the home is not located near the church.

Conflict may arise over exposure in the pastor's home especially if there are personality differences between the partners. His needs for more exposure and her needs for less (or vice versa) may clash. It is important that everyone's needs for exposure or privacy be appreciated and met as realistically as possible.

"I KNOW WHO YOU ARE, I THINK"

Tom was surprised by what Betty was saying and feeling: "I didn't think you felt that way." Tom's statement indicates that he, as well as Betty, may have inaccurate perceptions of the other. Probably Tom is projecting his own positive self-image onto Betty and is not aware of her feelings about herself and her world. Research has indicated that pastors and wives do have problems in perception of one another. However, this may be a common dilemma among the general populace. Tom had perceived that Betty was positive about her life as a parish pastor's wife. Betty may have assumed that Tom knew how she felt. Neither perception was accurate.

Tom and Betty's marriage is in trouble because their assumptions about one another have blocked paths of empathy in their daily communications. When they (or anyone else) harbor these mistaken assumptions, they miss each other's signals, and feelings of low self-esteem may become intensified.

Communications have broken down. Tom seems unaware that Betty feels neglected and that she is nursing low self-esteem and a battered self-image. Betty, operating daily in quiet desperation, lets some of her feelings out, only to be repressed by Tom's "things aren't that bad." She, misunderstood and denied the right to her own feelings, retreats into silence. Maybe Tom, expecting her to have it all together emotionally, operates on the assumption that he and his family should behave as a self-actualized, well-oiled machine. But marriage, like any living thing, needs maintenance and growth. Neither of them has acknowledged this, and both are barely coping. Betty will probably walk away again and Tom will dismiss the signs again.

The kind of coping that Tom and Betty do is characteristic of many marriages. It is like treading water to keep from drowning. But how long can it last? This is the opposite of growing, which is more like swimming. For swimmers, there is direction, there are goals, and there are islands along the way for refreshment and renewal.

Tom and Betty probably will not take advantage of marital growth opportunities. The Growth in Ministry research indicates that pastors verbally support marriage growth and enrichment opportunities but are themselves reluctant to participate lest the parishioners find out. The conclusion is that pastors tend to promote an image of a model marriage and that marriage enrichment is for sick marriages. But how long can any pastor's marriage go without serious attention?

SUMMARY AND POSTSCRIPTS

There are no simple formulas for dealing with the issues that have been discussed in this chapter, because each marriage and family is made up of unique persons with unique needs, desires, emotions, and behaviors. Each issue becomes a personal issue and a personal story.

Confusions about the spouse's role in the parish will have to be worked out by achieving a clear understanding of what is needed for a fulfilling life. Living solely out of others' expectations is inevitably counterproductive. Partners can begin working out a mutually satisfying relationship by first knowing themselves and being true to themselves as they dialogue in their relationships. Unconditional positive regard and an appreciation for one another become the building blocks for dealing with other issues. Once the issues are dealt with in the marriage relationship, the task of communicating the spouse's involvement in the parish becomes a mutual effort.

By developing an appropriate perspective on the use of time, the pastor has taken an essential step toward personal well-being and the well-being of the family. An inordinate response to the demands of the parish is a destructive way of dealing with marriage and family issues. The pastor may indeed value the ministry more than the marriage and the family. While this is unfortunate, it needs to be understood and worked out right there in the home.

It is safe to say that every person needs both private time and time for significant relationships. In order for this to happen in the pastor's marriage and family, it must be created intentionally. There must be time for self, time with spouse, and time with children. Families may set goals and negotiate contracts to assure time together, but even this will work only if accompanied by commitment and discipline.

Methods of support in a clergy marriage vary broadly. What is important, though, is understanding what support the other person needs and what they are willing and able to give. A partner may be asked to be a good listener in the home or a supporting presence in the parish. Pastors may be asked to support their partners by reinforcing discipline in the home or making accommodations in sharing family responsibilities because of the other's career. In either case, it is unfair to assume that each knows what the other's needs are without clearly asking the question, "How can I support you?"

Dealing with the public exposure that is characteristic of the pastor's home must be a team effort. Each person has unique needs for privacy and exposure. If a need for privacy is felt by one or the other partner, agreements can be made about when other persons are received and entertained in the home. Building a sensitivity about tolerable levels of exposure in yourself and your partner may increase satisfaction in the home. It is especially important for the pastor in a more traditional marriage to acknowledge that it is the wife who organizes and maintains the home, takes special pride in the home, and needs to know when the pastor-husband plans to entertain parish members and others in the home. In many circumstances intrusions into the home cannot be predicted. But it is important to realize that the home is an essential component to a couple's privacy.

An accurate understanding of each other requires honest dialogue if it is to grow beyond projections of one's own feelings. It involves a commitment of time, privacy, and a concerted effort to listen to each other. There are numerous programs and tools available today which are designed to develop communication skills and increase one's ability to communicate feelings in appropriate ways and to deal with the feelings of others without threat.

The chapter has addressed issues in the pastor's marriage and family in a piecemeal fashion. In order to pull the discussion together in a wholistic approach to marriage and family, the notion of a "chain of compatibility" is valuable. Spiritual, sexual, and interpersonal relationships form this chain within marriage. When there are breakdowns in any of these aspects of marriage, the other aspects are affected. Sexual problems affect the total relationship, because the deep spiritual and interpersonal aspects of our lives are an integrated total and cannot be fragmented and left inside the bedroom door. This goes for all aspects. What is essential to the process of discovering and rediscovering each other are the attitudes which are brought into the marriage and nurtured. Acknowledging that there is a chain of compatibility that transcends any one of the components broadens one's appreciation of human relationships and helps us understand ourselves more clearly. Mere performance or focus on one or two aspects cannot nurture the whole person. A desire for a wholistic approach to life is seen as a strong desire for many pastors and their spouses. But before this can be realized in daily life, the couple must contend with those taboos against acknowledging marital pressures and problems and resist trying to live fragile myths which claim that there are perfect marriages. The credo of any healthy marriage must affirm that there is grace in growth.

When I first sat down to write this concluding chapter, I had a very different idea in mind than what I ended up with. But the more I thought about what the future may bring to the ministry, the more I became convinced that it was futile to predict any specifics. But if what the futurists are saying is any indication, we had best be prepared to begin understanding our ministries in terms of the monumental pressures the next few years may bring. This chapter emphasizes the need for a strong sense of community in our congregations. It seems to me that we should begin exploring as never before just what the congregational community can and should be. Will the so-called family nights and other traditional fellowship offerings be sufficient to provide our people with the strong sense of community and nurture they may need in order to cope? I doubt it. The folks who come to fellowship events are likely to be the folks who are already coping. I don't offer any strategies here for accomplishing an intensified community. I don't have any terrific ideas on the subject. Yet I think we'd best work at developing these strategies. Probably the seeds for these strategies were sown in the earlier chapters. Lest I come off sounding pessimistic, though, let me add that while I think that the future will be a difficult time, I also think it will be a remarkably exciting time for us who minister in and to it.—*Editor*

11

Community as Future

THOMAS E. KADEL

Sometimes I don't feel much like God's representative to anything. Just try to feel special while standing and waiting for the steam to clear from the bathroom mirror after the morning shower. There I am, naked, hair a blasted mess, a day's growth of beard, and a night's growth of bad breath.

Somewhere, someone who should, it seems, feel like a representative of God is intoning Lauds to himself or someone. But here I am, as naked and defenseless and repulsive as I'll be all day long, waiting for the steam to go away so I can see if I'm still the same person I put to bed last night.

Somewhere, the person who ought to be called a minister is intoning, "O Lord, open thou my lips and my mouth shall show forth thy praise."

Here in this bathroom, if I could sing anything it would likely be "O Lord, open thou my lips and my mouth shall blow forth bad breath."

Years ago in a North Carolina church, I stood awestruck with a group of my classmates at our ordination service. The synod president asked us, "Are you ready to take upon you this holy ministry, and faithfully to serve therein?"

Dutifully and with great devotion we each answered, "Yes, by the help of God."

If that synod president were standing here in my bathroom right now, fully robed and still trying to keep his lavaliere microphone from clanging into his massive pectoral cross as he asked, "Are you ready . . . ?" I'm not sure what I'd answer.

There's no sense, large or small, in which I feel holy or set apart this morning. I'm not sure I'm ready for anything . . . least of all to take upon me "this holy ministry."

Which one of us did God call to ministry? Did he call the awestruck young man, full of confidence and faith? Or did he call this stranger who is beginning to look back at me from the steamed mirror?

In spite of myself, I'd have to answer that he probably called the latter. I can't explain why, but that's my conviction. That imperfect, unshaven borderline heretic is the one who's on the line today to be someone called a pastor.

Scratch most ministers and you will find right below the surface a person who shouldn't be God's representative. We've seen too much of ourselves; we know too much about ourselves that those trusting saints out there would never suspect; and we have fears that no person who has taken on "this holy ministry" ought to harbor. But, that's us. This is the gang that God has called together to point to the holy. And quivering fingers and all, that's what we'll be doing today—mostly.

Who is this group of people who are called by the rather awesome title of Reverend? What is to be their role in the coming years? How might we expect that role to change or modify? These are difficult questions, and no one has specific answers. We can, however, cite some of the trends and forces at work on the ministry and the people ministered to and make some educated guesses.

My goal is not to lay out a detailed program for what to do to make ministry better in the next years. It is rather to consider what some of our most important needs might be and how men and women who know deep down that they are just like everyone else might still function in "this holy ministry."

BEING A SACRAMENT

A few years ago a woman's struggle changed much about the way that I understand my ministry, and she may have pointed me toward one of the great needs of the future. It was a cold Maundy Thursday afternoon and we were having services for the older folks who couldn't come out at night. There were only a dozen or so of us there and I was pretty discouraged by the attendance, feeling that if I'm going to all this trouble to have an extra service, others ought to have the courtesy to come.

Sally had come, though, and she had brought all of the incredible burdens she carried with her. She was a deeply troubled woman who hadn't known a day of real peace since long before I first met her. I always felt uncomfortable with Sally because nothing ever cheered her up, and that's part of how I understood my job. I was the professional cheerer-upper. She was proof that I wasn't perfect.

When it came time to celebrate the Sacrament of the Altar, we stood around a makeshift table in a room which was more accessible to the weak of limb. I thought I noticed it when I came to her with the bread. "Sally, the Body of Christ, given for you." Something about her looked different. Shortly I was back with the wine. "Sally, this is the Blood of Christ, shed for you." It was there again, that look.

A day or so later while I visited with her, I suddenly saw the same look again. "Pastor, do you remember Maundy Thursday?"

"Sure."

"I have never felt such peace as came over me while we stood around that altar." Her eyes began to fill with tears. "God was there, wasn't he?"

"Of course he was, Sally." Those were my words, but I'm not sure I believed them until I saw how he really *had* been there for her. I was merely "working my job" that day and was upset that my plans hadn't been fulfilled better. She was there seeing what Augustine called "the visible Word of God."

The only thing that's more frightening than reading Alvin Toffler's book *Future Shock*[15] is to hear him say more recently that he was wrong. Now he admits that he entirely underestimated the quickness and the strength with which the future would crash into people.

Sally was one of the future's victims. It ran over her like a jet-powered steamroller. She couldn't cope. She was also a prototype of what some are predicting for more and more of us in the future: harried, hassled, confused, and struggling from one moment's crisis to the next. But somehow, for that one magic moment on a cold Maundy Thursday afternoon, God slowed things down for Sally. He became a sacrament for her and she could see him, feel him, and taste him. The Word became visible and it brought peace.

Bernard Cooke in *Ministry to Word and Sacraments*[16] asserts that in a sense there are more than two sacraments. He says that whenever the Word becomes visible, we experience the sacramental presence of God.

Part of understanding oneself to be a minister (as Mark Rouch so beautifully put it in chapter nine) is to understand oneself as a potential sacrament, an earthly element through which the Word becomes visible to another. Ordained clergy, though, do not have a monopoly on this. It belongs first and foremost to God's people, the community of believers. The leader of that community of the sacrament becomes something of a sacrament within a sacrament, as does each member as they make the Word visible to each other by allowing moments of blessing to happen between them.

In my understanding of the future, nothing seems to scream out as loudly for our attention as the need for us to become visible Word to each other and collectively to the world. It is our job to present ourselves to God that he might use us to momentarily slow the world down for that moment of blessing. In the preceding pages some well-informed people have shared their thoughts about strategies that might be useful—not for becoming ministers, but for removing some of the obstacles which we place in the way of God using us as sacraments.

As we look a bit into the future, there are indications that how we understand ourselves and our ministries may make big differences to those we serve. We'll still be the folks with the bad morning breath waiting for the steam to clear from the bathroom mirror. But if the Lord can use some of the simply awful wines I've tasted at the altar, he can also use us. If he can use home-baked loaves that crumble to the touch to bring grace, he can use us even when we are about to crumble from the strain of competing demands.

THE EROSION OF THE WE

One cannot stand and peer through the doorway to the final two decades of this century without feeling that the Western life-style is in for some radical changes. Energy problems, unpaid social bills, certain technological advances and declines, the feminization of society, the structure and function of families, and other concerns which are with us today will, I believe, continue to seriously call into question the nature of community.

This has certainly already begun. We've moved consistently from the development of the "I've gotta be me" philosophy of the sixties through the "I've gotta get mine" philosophy of the seventies. Observers have periodically tried to compare the liberalism of the sixties with the growing conservatism of the seventies. In one sense, these philosophies are actually the same thing. They look different, to be sure, but inside they are built of the same stuff—the erosion of the WE.

The human community, so bounced and battered by its attempts to deal with the ever-quickening pace of life, has lost much of its communal consciousness. Self-identity groups are becoming smaller and smaller in their inclusiveness. As the pace of life and its accompanying survival tactics rub people together more and more, little pieces of the community fall off and begin developing their identity in contrast to all the rest. For years this tendency toward specialization was observable in certain professions like law and medicine. But at the same time, much less noticed, society began to specialize as well.

Some of the examples are obvious. Once upon a time, the great divisions were between the old and the young, the white and the black, the rich and the poor. But now we have witnessed the grays pulling away from the salt and peppers, the professionals (both black and white) pulling further away from the nonprofessionals, the singles pulling away from the marrieds, the childless couples from those with children, gays pulling away from straights, and enlightened women pulling away from unenlightened men. The list could go on and on.

None of these groups sat down and decided to pull away from

others. The question was not factionalism but survival. It was not so much intentional as it was necessary. By specializing, society's members began looking for the lowest common denominator. Specialization seemed to give groups a clearer voice with the rest of society. It also, and perhaps more importantly, afforded an identity. Power politics was the name we gave to it, power identity-building was what was really happening.

The church was not left unaffected by this search for these smaller identity groups. The ecumenism of the sixties made it unacceptable to accentuate the different identities between denominations, but it opened other doors. Push one bubble down and it will pop up someplace else. Some identity groups began to express themselves within denominations. Others left and began operating as separate denominations. Still others dropped out and drew their identities from being antidenominational. To be sure, there were some weighty issues, such as freedom, perception of the work of the Spirit, ways of interpreting Scripture, and more. But the need for a specialized identity apart from the general community was a major factor in much of this.

As the pace and complexity of life increases, so does the apparent need to band together in even smaller groups that can help individuals preserve a sense of their own identity and purpose. There are no real signs that this is abating. The predictions are that these stresses will continue and intensify.

WHAT'S AHEAD?

A whole new science has grown up in recent years and is led by folks called futurists. They have accepted the challenge of tracing present trends and plotting future possibilities and options. What they say is sometimes frightening. Most futurists foresee a fire storm of changes slamming into cultures which are unprepared to deal with them. Many predict profound changes as family structure and function continue to evolve; as society feminizes (both in terms of women's participation and in society's make-over with more traditional feminine values and characteristics); as significant changes happen in the role and use of leisure time; and in a wide-sweeping evolution of new values systems.

Recently we have witnessed the beginning of a profound change in society's approach to change. Up to now, the essential question has been "Is it possible?" Beginning mostly in grass-roots movements, a new question is being asked: "Is it preferable?" Certain futurists like Toffler maintain that this question may be the key to the future sanity of society, if not to its survival.

Another related aspect which is certain to grab our attention is the continued proliferation of choices. Seen as a luxury and an earmark of our advanced society, some futurists and social scientists are beginning to question whether we really need all of these choices. Does having, as someone suggested, literally twenty-five million choices between all the makes, styles, and options of automobiles contribute to our affluence and freedom? Or does it contribute to our feelings of helplessness and overload?

Some issues that futurists deal with are so new that new words had to be coined to describe them. *Future shock, technocracy,* and *ecospasm* are words that have begun creeping into the general vocabulary. One of the more descriptive of the new words is *adhocracy,* which is a crisis-to-crisis method of leadership characterized by the establishment of temporary task forces and ad hoc groups. Adhocracy is a strategy for those engaged in the short-term question of survival. It is becoming a standard mode of operation in government, in many families, and in congregations.

The church, unless it chooses obsolescence, will have to deal with these earmarks of the future. It must discover ways to help its people adjust and survive this onslaught. But more than that, it is called on to assist society. The twin roles of prophet and priest will be challenged, perhaps as never before, to interpret the faith in terms of unavoidable changes and to minister to those left behind in a heap.

THE COMMUNITY UNDER STRESS

Clergy have found themselves for the past thirty-five years in the middle of all these changes, and their job description has changed significantly. Among Lutheran clergy there has been a change in orientation from theologian to practitioner. I suspect that part of the reason for this has been the desire to meet needs which were being expressed more and more by the various groups within a single congregation. The pastor's work has been described as being a generalist. It is probably more like being a specialist to the various specialized needs and wants of the people.

Someday soon the pastor may need to develop specialties for use with the energy users on one hand and the energy savers on the other; with those firmly rooted in a satisfying identity group and those casting about for one; between those who are the adapters to rapid change and those who are its victims. The pastor may indeed find that within his or her own congregation there will be those whose survival and comfort increasingly depend on the defeat and discomfort of others.

If this seems too far out, consider society as a whole today. Those in nuclear-related occupations depend on the defeat of those who fear nuclear energy. Those who strike for higher wages cause discomfort for those who must purchase the higher-priced goods. Those who cherish traditional values depend on the submission of those who champion new ones.

One of the strengths of the church has been that the laborer has sat next to the vice-president of the company, the auto worker next to the woman who just purchased a new car, the "swinging single" next to the devoted family man, and the ecologist next to the strip miner.

People do not have to be alike in order to stand before the same God. This ministry in the midst of diversity will continue to be the strength of the church, but it may require greater intentionality on the community's part. As the pace of life continues to quicken and as more and more small groups are rubbed off, the challenge to the Christian community will grow more intense.

THE COMMUNITY AS SACRAMENT

But while there are factors pulling us apart, there are others pulling us together. We need a place and a people to trust. We need a place where some traditions and conventions remain essentially the same from year to year. We need a place where we can be blessed and can be a blessing to others. We need a place where we can see and taste something which transcends the daily anxieties. Specifically, we need a place where we can be sacramented and can sacrament others, a place where the Word becomes visible and dwells among us, a place where we can be transformed from the earthly element we know ourselves to be into the holy element we'd really like to be to someone else.

Perhaps the greatest task facing the future Christian community and those who serve as ministers within that community is to help us recognize and long for those moments of blessing. In this sense, the ministry of Word and Sacrament may take on a whole new meaning to those who have been captured by its promise. We've technologized the meaning of Word and Sacrament to the point where the words speak of specific tasks accomplished by God, participated in by ordained clergy, and handed to the laity. The Word is the well-read lection or the well-written and provocative sermon. The Sacrament is either Holy Baptism or Holy Communion. We have soldered these concepts to the circuit board of the church, making their functions rigid and well-defined. We've defined what happens when they are there and what happens when they are absent. We've robbed them of their independent and magical life.

But the Word began not as a transistor, but as a promise. The Sacrament began not as a capacitor, but as the visible working of that promise. The Christian community began not as a circuit board perpetually producing the same signal, but as a living body needing both to receive the sacramental presence of God and to pass it along to others.

If the world of future shock has need of anything, it has need of the sacramental presence of this community, a community which not only speaks God's blessing to it but allows itself to be transformed into that blessing. Too often in the past we have withdrawn the sacrament from the world by trying to remove ourselves from it or by speaking only the word of judgment to it.

But in the years to come the world will need this blessing

more than ever. The world will need to see people who believe in magic and who are insane enough to invite others to believe in it as well. It will need to have the hem of the blessed garment pass close enough that they may reach out and touch it.

But the Christian community is made up of people who are in the first place people of this same world—people who need the same things that everybody else needs. Therefore the community will come back to itself time and again to be sacramented by God through the ministers of their own community. One or two of those ministers may be ordained. Most will not be. We've begun calling what happens within that community nurture. That literally means "to supply with nourishment." It also means making the Word visible and tasteable to one another. It means being used as a sacrament to one another—nourishing each other with our care and our love and our dependence upon the promise.

ORDAINED MINISTRY—A FUTURE?

I've been suggesting that what the futurists see coming our way will compel the church to take more seriously than ever the community aspect of its life. There within that community will come the nurture and the moments of blessing that will make adjustment to the future more possible. But with the stronger emphasis on community, what happens to the role that the ordained minister will assume? As the fog clears from the bathroom mirror, will the minister see the face of a dinosaur, an obsolete entity who is carried for reasons of tradition instead of function?

I think that quite the contrary will happen. The role of the ordained minister will change. But if anything it will become even more important—not because the ministers themselves are so special, but because what their office symbolizes will be what the community needs to see.

Despite much talk to the contrary, most lay people and clergy essentially see the ordained ministry as superior to lay ministry. There has for many of us been something of a frustration that a call to a shut-in somehow "counts more" if it is made by the pastor. I for one saw this as a symptom of people's perception of my ministry as more important than theirs. I was convinced this was their way of neglecting their own ministries. I may have been partially right. But there was another whole dimension which I overlooked. It is this dimension which will grow in importance in the years to come.

The ordained minister should be one who stands in the midst of this new community. He or she is never separate from it or superior to it. But the ordained minister accepts the additional task of being the symbol of the life of the congregation. This symbol is most obvious as the pastor becomes worship leader and celebrant of the sacraments. But the pastor is additionally symbolic of the congregation's life together.

The pastor is there at the time of birth and the time of death. The pastor is there during moments of crisis and of joy. He or she is there because the entire community of faith cannot be there. Ordination does not mean that the pastor can bring a greater portion of God to the person on the deathbed. Anyone who is there in love is there in God's name and in God's power. But the pastor can symbolize the concern and love of the entire people, the community. He or she becomes the visible Word of God as expressed through the community of believers and brings the moment of blessing in *their* names and in *God's* name. The pastor is there not because of a commission from the church hierarchy but because of one from the community.

The ordained pastor is not, then, some special envoy sent directly from God. That would be more of a burden than most of us could bear. But that notion persists. That notion compels the pastor to be someone different than the community and to bring that differentness along in a briefcase and distribute it to others. But that notion will be of very little help to the people of the future community. Even if the pastor is able to survive future shock, it means only that the "special people" can do it. The "regular people" draw no courage from that.

The pastor must minister from within the community, the very community that would be encouraged to know of our early-morning struggles in the bathroom. They would be encouraged because that is also their struggle. Each member of the community of faith must face the person in the mirror who has been called to serve and to witness and to point to the holy. That early-morning struggle is the community's struggle. Clergy who have no monopoly on ministering can draw some comfort that they also have no monopoly on the struggle to be a blessing to others.

Sometimes I don't feel like God's representative to anything. And those times are the most authentic times. The community of faith is God's representative. I, as the ordained minister, am the community's representative. "This holy ministry," as the ordination service puts it, is the ministry of all of us who are called by God to be his people. The early-morning struggle in the bathroom confirms that for me again and again, if I'll catch it. It is not that *I* am different, but that *we* are.

In the end, the future of the ordained ministry will still be about the old and senile man awaiting a visit from a pastor he won't recognize. It will remain endless committee meetings and administrations. It will still be motivated as often by guilt as by commitment. It will still be simultaneously haunted and blessed by images of a cross flashing past our mind's eye at the most inappropriate moments. It will remain helping people grow when, it seems, they've already outgrown us in some of the things that really matter. It will remain quick touches to the forehead to see if the ashes have blown off yet. It will remain the building of tabernacles on magic mountains only to see the mountain hiccup and knock them off. It will remain all of these things.

But most of all, the ministry will remain God's as expressed through a future-shocked community gathered in his name for those sacred moments of blessing. It will remain God's as, by some miracle, that same community is empowered to go outside itself to be visible Word to others who are beaten up just as badly. It will remain God's ministry as that community expresses itself through one who fears the morning look in the mirror because he knows he can't do the job. Somehow, though, through that same miracle, he does.

Notes

1. The recommendations for dealing with conflict which are presented here are Dr. Dittes' own as developed in his book *When People Say No* (New York: Harper & Row, Publishers, 1979).
2. P. T. Forsyth, *Positive Preaching and the Modern Mind* (1907; first American printing, Grand Rapids: William B. Eerdmans Publishing Co., 1966), p. 28. Used by permission.
3. R. L. Rubenstein (as quoted by Jack H. Bloom, "Who Became Clergymen?" *Journal of Religion and Health* 10, no. 1 [January 1971]: 51), "The Clergy and Psychoanalysis," *Reconstructionist* 1966. Used by permission.
4. Daniel Zeluff, *There's Algae in the Baptismal Font* (Nashville: Abingdon Press, 1978), p. 29. Used by permission.
5. Anton T. Boisen, *The Exploration of the Inner World* (New York: Harper & Row, Publishers, 1936), p. 285. Used by permission.
6. Frank W. Klos, *Confirmation and First Communion* (Philadelphia: Board of Publication, Lutheran Church in America, 1968), pp. 53–54.
7. Henri Nouwen, *Creative Ministry* (Garden City, N.Y.: Doubleday & Co., 1971).
8. Joseph Sittler, *The Ecology of Faith* (Philadelphia: Muhlenberg Press, 1961; paperback edition Fortress Press, 1970), p. 83.
9. Mark A. Rouch, *Competent Ministry: A Guide to Effective Continuing Education* (Nashville: Abingdon Press, 1974). See especially chapters 1–3.
10. Ibid., pp. 16–17.
11. Wolfhart Pannenberg, *Jesus: God and Man* (Philadelphia: Westminster Press, 1974).
12. Sister Marlene Helpin, a presentation at the annual meeting of the Society for the Advancement of Continuing Education for Ministry, Atlanta, Ga., June 1978.
13. SACEM, 855 Locust St., Collegeville, Pa. 19426.
14. For regional catalogs of continuing education program agencies and what they offer, write to SACEM at the address noted above.
15. Alvin Toffler, *Future Shock* (New York: Random House, 1970).
16. Bernard Cooke, *Ministry to Word and Sacraments* (Philadelphia: Fortress Press, 1976; paperback edition, 1980).

DATE DUE